DRIVING
HORSE-DRAWN CARRIAGES
FOR PLEASURE

THE CLASSIC
ILLUSTRATED GUIDE
TO COACHING, HARNESSING,
STABLING, ETC.

Francis T. Underhill

DOVER PUBLICATIONS, INC.
New York

Published in Canada by General Publishing Company, Ltd., 30 Lesmill Road, Don Mills, Toronto, Ontario.

Published in the United Kingdom by Constable and Company, Ltd.

This Dover edition, first published in 1989, is an unabridged, slightly altered republication of the work originally published in 1897 by D. Appleton and Company, New York, with the title *Driving for Pleasure; or, The Harness Stable and Its Appointments.* Some of the illustrations have been moved from their original positions.

Manufactured in the United States of America
Dover Publications, Inc., 31 East 2nd Street, Mineola, N.Y. 11501

Library of Congress Cataloging-in-Publication Data

Underhill, Francis T.
[Driving for pleasure]
Driving horse-drawn carriages for pleasure : the classic illustrated guide to coaching, harnessing, stabling, etc. / Francis T. Underhill.
p. cm.
Reprint. Originally published: Driving for pleasure. New York : D. Appleton, 1897.
ISBN 0-486-26102-6
1. Driving of horse drawn vehicles. 2. Coaching. 3. Driving of horse drawn vehicles—Equipment and supplies. 4. Carriages and carts. I. Title.
SF305.U55 1989
798'.6—dc20   89-30500
                                 CIP

PREFACE.

THE want of a book which treats directly of the proper appointment of sporting and nonsporting vehicles has prompted the preparation of this work.

The numerous horse shows held throughout the country have developed a desire for information among the onlookers, as well as among those who drive actively and passively, without the possibility of satisfying it except through the medium of the obliging friend who, in nine cases out of ten, speaks without knowledge.

It is believed also that this desire for exact information regarding appointments, horses, harness and harnessing, bits and bitting, the stable, and other kindred matters, is shared by a very large number of owners of one, two, or three horses who wish their stables and equipages, however modest, to be appointed correctly and in accordance with the dictates of practical experience.

It may not be out of place to say that the author's

qualifications for this task include not only twenty years of driving, but also a long service as judge at horse shows, which has furnished unlimited opportunities for the study and comparison of equipages. The results of the lessons which he has learned, the errors which he has noted, and the points of special merit which have come to his attention while passing in review thousands of equipages, have very naturally furnished unusual advantages for the preparation of a book which has been undertaken with some hesitation, and yet in a belief founded on experience that a work of this kind is greatly needed.

In the endeavour to consider each subject without partiality, every available means of obtaining the necessary authentic information has been employed.

Differences of opinion among experts have necessitated extra work in many instances; in such cases the standard described has been selected from the authorities whose arguments seemed most reasonable and practical.

Without attempting the laying down of inflexible rules, the intent has been to suggest rather than to dictate.

Availability for the illustration of such points as were under discussion has been considered in some cases at the expense of perfect detail.

The sincere thanks of the author are due to the friends who have enabled him to secure the necessary photographs, often at much trouble to themselves.

F. T. U.

NEW YORK, *October 1, 1896.*

CONTENTS.

INDEX TO ILLUSTRATIONS.

DRIVING FOR PLEASURE.

CHAPTER I.

WHAT CONSTITUTES "GOOD FORM" IN EQUIPAGE.

SIMPLICITY of outline, appropriateness, consistency, harmony, and good judgment in the selection of vehicles, form the foundation of what may be termed good form.

The selection of vehicles is mentioned, because that is practically the basis of operation. Each vehicle demands consistency in the choice of its horses, servants, harness, livery, etc., and simplicity in its design and treatment, resulting in that much-to-be-desired harmony of the whole.

A good carriage is intended for many years of hard use, and not to be thrown aside, like a woman's gown, in obedience to the dictates of any and every whim of so-called fashion. The same may be said of a well-kept harness; and all this goes to show how important it is that the first choice should be carefully made.

1

Of course, there are many incidental details which
are factors, and which are liable to some slight change
from time to time. The silk hat, for example, although looked upon with favour to-day, may be considered absurd ten years hence. An avoidance of
extremes in all such trifles will keep one within limits
for many a long day.

One occasionally sees an equipage belonging to
elderly people; the carriage evidently an old one, but
in good condition and on good lines; the servants
respectable-looking men past middle age; the horses
sleek and well cared for, and possibly adorned with
flowing tails—the whole effect savouring of what one
might call the days gone by. Such an establishment
is in far better form for its purpose than one which
shows in its every detail that it has but recently
come into existence.

It is unfortunate that we have so few examples
of this type in America, but the fact is, very few of
our coach-builders of a past generation approached
the foreign-built carriages in design, so that almost
all the good carriages of that period were imported,
and the importations were not numerous; besides
which, the then condition of our roads and streets
was not favourable to heavy vehicles.

Young people, of course, must be equally consistent,
and select carriages somewhat suited to their years.

They should be more thorough also, for, while a slight deficiency in the grandfather's carriage might be overlooked, such leniency can not be extended to the younger generation, for they have advantages which their grandfathers did not possess.

Money, that god which seems to be so much worshipped to-day, has a tendency to incline its possessors toward a display and flashiness in equipage which is distinctly bad form.

To this source can be traced most of the shoddy "turnouts" which constitute far too large a proportion of our private establishments. Such people can give their pockets quite as much relief, and at the same time contribute to their pleasure and amusement, by running an extensive stable and doing it smartly.

Americans are known as a most adaptive race, and when once the appreciation of a good thing is inculcated, the improvement achieved is extraordinary. So let it be with good form in equipage.

CHAPTER II.

GENERAL APPOINTMENTS.

THE preceding chapter is designed to point out the necessity of adhering to simplicity, combined with as much symmetry of outline as is possible, in every variety of carriage.

This simplicity should be carried out in the harness, livery, etc. The owner, if his means allow, can produce a brilliant effect by means of uncommonly good horseflesh. What can look worse than a poorly designed and gaudily painted brougham with enormous, fantastically shaped lamps resembling those used on the Lord Mayor's coach of yore? The whole tawdry effect is generally emphasized by an elaborate harness replete with enormous monograms, and partially hiding a pair of "screws" which would disgrace a street car.

The contrast between such an equipage, and the perfectly-turned-out brougham, which is so quiet in design and treatment as to be almost unnoticeable, is very great. In this case the harness is plain but handsomely made; the servants are clad in smart, well-fitting and *well-put-on* liveries; they carry themselves

4

with an air of pride, and seem to feel that the effect of their equipage depends on them—as in a great measure it does.

With such appointments, a carriage will at least look respectable when drawn by even an ordinary pair; and when the horses are really fine and thoroughly adapted to their work, the effect produced will compel the admiration of the intelligent on-looker, although in most cases he will not know what attracts him. This, then, is the ideal which should guide those who wish to turn out really well.

The colouring of a carriage has much to do with its general effect. Plain black, and the dark shades of green, blue, and claret, produce the best results in carriages for town use of the non-sporting class. Bright-coloured wheels and undercarriages should never be attempted unless the owner be more than ordinarily well versed in the remainder of the appointments. A departure such as this requires the extreme of severity in treatment to make it pass muster.

In England, of course, where family colours have been in use for generations, the conditions are somewhat different, but the family whose colours are quiet is to be congratulated.

Unless a wheel is of good design, a plain colour will emphasize its defects. In fact, it is often by this means that the uncultivated eye is brought to distinguish between the good and the bad in carriage designing.

A well-made harness is often spoiled by excessive ornamentation—gorgeous monograms or crests covering every available surface. Oftentimes the same decorations reduced one half in size would look perfectly proper.

For wet-weather driving, the smartest possible harness is made of black leather throughout, with the metal parts covered. Of course, such a harness as this must be well designed and appropriately used.

Good liveries are essential to a well-appointed equipage; and yet no department is as much neglected in this country. When one has seen the same carriage, well turned out in other respects, either improved or ruined by smart or slouchy servants, he will appreciate the point.

The very position of the servants contributes largely toward the general finish. Put a slouchy mustached coachman on the box of the best generally appointed carriage procurable, and its good points go for naught. No private coachman wears a mustache or beard, and the presence of such can invariably be considered an indication of ignorance of his calling. Such a man may be a good strapper, and in a general-utility place might be satisfactory; but he should never be employed as a coachman.

The town coachman must be a man of experience, and reasonable wages paid to such a man will often save a large expenditure in paint and repairs. The thorough coachman can be distinguished at a glance, and it is unfortunate that they are so few and far between.

CHAPTER III.

COACHING.

Ah, what a charm that word has to the man who is really an enthusiast! It requires a knowledge of the highest branches of the art of horsemanship and equipage to insure a satisfactory result. It is a sport that has come down to us from the days of the old English stage and mail coaches, before the introduction of the railway.

In those days, a number of amateurs, whose names are familiar to all readers of coaching history, were in the habit of driving some of the regular coaches whenever the opportunity offered, and educated as they were under the very best professional whips of the then time, they acquired a practical appreciation of the points necessary to a master of the art.

When we consider to-day the speed at which some of the fast mails were run, we must realize that the men who drove them thoroughly understood their business. The Edinburgh mail, for instance, ran four hundred miles in forty hours, including stoppages. At first glance, an average of ten miles an hour will not seem a very fast rate; but when we appreciate that the time occupied in changing horses, in stopping for meals, etc., is included in the schedule—which means that the coaches must have maintained a running speed of practically fourteen miles an hour, and that over roads which, though good, were far inferior to the English roads of to-day, through storm and sunshine, by day and night, with nothing to steady the coach on a downward incline but the wheelers and a skid—we are convinced that those coachmen were by right the past masters from whom the disciples of coaching must acquire a great portion of their knowledge.

When the days of public coaches were at an end, and most of the famous professional whips were forced to give up the "bench," or to assume a more modest one than that of the road coach, the amateurs took up the ball of coaching enthusiasm and kept it rolling; and it is in a great measure through them that we are enabled to-day to be almost in touch with many of the famous old traditions of the road.

Some portion of their knowledge and experience has been transmitted by means of the pen, but in a very great measure the niceties of the art have been passed down through the medium of the real enthusiast.

A few—a very few—individuals in each succeeding generation, have gone into the work with a thorough appreciation of its nice points. They have, as young men, given the closest attention to the instruction afforded them by the representatives of the art in the generation previous, and in due course have themselves become the mentors of the rising generation.

It is only within the past quarter of a century that Americans have fallen into line in the pursuit of this sport. There were, of course, many gentlemen in this country long prior to that time who derived a certain amount of pleasure from four-in-hand driving, but very few acquired what might be termed "masterly coachmanship."

Although it may be very justly contended that many of the little fads which are advocated by experts of the school of to-day do not in any way contribute directly to the actual improvement of driving, they nevertheless serve to interest, and thereby keep the mind of the coachman more thoroughly concentrated on a proper indulgence in and perpetuation of the sport.

Outsiders often criticise the copying in our coaches of a vehicle which belonged to more primitive days. They forget, however, that although the outlines of the vehicles are similar, those of to-day have been enor-

Plate 1: Park Drag.

Plate II: Park Drag "Turned Out."

mously improved by means of the increased skill in coachbuilding.

The modern park drag or road coach can not be said to be adapted to use on many of our sandy country roads, and in districts where such prevail a vehicle better suited to the purpose must perforce be used. But be it remembered, also, that sandy roads themselves are gradually becoming more and more a relic of the past.

There may be said to be two methods of indulging in the sport of coaching to-day.

First, the driving of a coach or drag simply for the amusement of the owner and his friends.

Second, the running of a "public" or road coach.

The gentlemen's drag differs quite considerably in many points from the road coach, and the rules of the coaching club, which are quoted herewith, point out the distinctions.

THE PARK DRAG.

The park drag, as shown in Plate I, is an excellent type of a proper vehicle. Plate II shows the turning out of the same. The drag in this case lacks a little, in that mail axles take the place of Collinge's; the latter savour a little more of the refinement which belongs to the park drag. The harness is described in the chapter on Harness and Harnessing, and needs no further comment. This may also be said of the liveries, etc.

It is well to remember that when a drag is brought to the owner's door or is on exhibition the lazybacks of the gammon and back gammon—viz., the front and back roof seats—should be turned down, and remain so in case the only passenger is carried on the box seat beside the coachman.

Plate III shows the servants in the position of ascending the hind seat, and is simply intended to impress the necessity of having one's grooms carry out a certain uniformity of action. (The costume of the coachman in this picture demands an apology.)

Plates IV and V show the distinction between the rear view of a park drag and that of a road coach, and it is from this point of view that the difference is probably most noticeable. The hind boot in the park drag is hinged at the bottom, so that, when dropped, it forms a table for the serving of luncheon, etc.; in the road coach it is hinged on the off side, to allow of the guard having easy access to it from the near hind step when the coach is in motion. It will be noticed that the skid is hung on the off side, while in England it is carried on the near side. This change has been made necessary by the American rules of the road, which oblige one to turn to the right.

Plate III: Servants ascending Hind Seat of Park Drag.

Plate IV : Rear View of Park Drag.

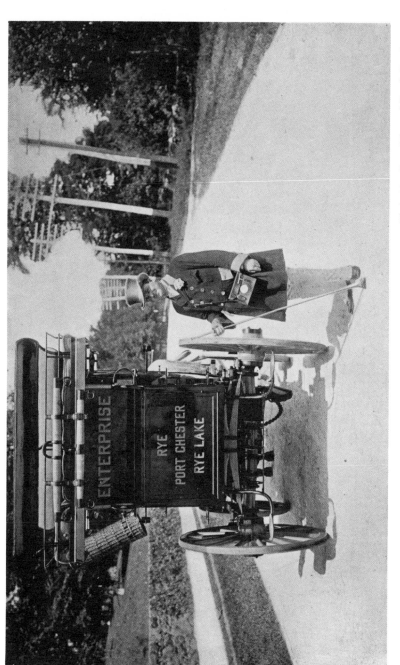

Plate V: Rear View of Road Coach, with Guard in Livery.

Plate VI: Drag or Coach "Parked."

And so one might go on through the various distinctions which are carefully portrayed in the photographs, but such a minute description would be verbose and unnecessary.

It is the aim of every good coachman to have a sound argument in support of all the little technicalities, and it may afford the reader interested in the subject some amusement to examine in detail the differences which exist between the park drag and the road coach, and, after analyzing them, to draw his own conclusions.

Plate VI shows the drag "parked" for the races or similar use. The coach should always be in this position when the horses are out, except when in the coach room.

THE PRIVATE ROAD COACH.

Plate VII shows a park drag as turned out for private road use, or, in other words, for use in the country or on coaching trips.

The servants wear their stable clothes, as full liveries are not at all adapted to such a purpose; the harness is of the road order, and it is customary to attach a luggage rail to the roof, so that any luggage, rugs, etc., may be safely carried there. The horn case is strapped to the rail on the off side, so that it can be conveniently within the reach of the head groom, who is generally the one to sound it in case of need. (By the way, one never speaks of "blowing" or "blowing on" the horn.) This is not necessary, however, for it is generally wisest to carry the horn in the basket, mouthpiece up, most horns having shifting mouthpieces which are liable to slip off when the horn is put in the case, and for this reason the case is really only intended as a protection to the horn when in the coach house. The photograph also shows the position of the loin cloths, and is equally proper to the road coach. (The cloth on the off wheeler is improperly folded.)

ROAD COACHING.

Plates VIII and IX show very good examples of the genus road coach. As in the case of the park drag, all its essentials are described in the coaching-club rules and will need no further comment.

Plates X and XI show the cockhorse "alone" and "put to." The details are sufficiently clear in the photograph to require no additional description. The harness would be somewhat more proper were the hames without terrets, and were the bridle provided with blinkers and more on the harness order. It will be noticed that the bar is connected with the pole head by a rope which has a solid eye in one end and a spring

Plate VII : Private Road Coach.

Plate VIII : Public Road Coach.

Plate IX: Road Coach "Turned Out."

Plate X : Cockhorse and Boy.

Plate XI: Public Coach with Cockhorse.

cockeye in the other. The end with the eye is slipped over the pole hook and rests on top of that of the leaders' main bar; the other end is then passed between the leaders and through a large ring suspended by straps from their kidney link rings, after which it is snapped in the eye of the cockhorse's bar.

A few suggestions as to the necessities in the "putting on" of a road coach may not be amiss. We will suppose the route to have been selected, the distance, variety of the road, etc., ascertained.

The usual allowance for a well-run road coach is one horse to the mile, which allowance should run the same coach both ways on a short route, and a coach each way on a long one. On a thirty-mile route thirty horses should take the coach sixty miles. On a route of the above length it is customary to run each way daily with the same coach. The proper staging of the horses is a very important consideration, and one on which it will be difficult to lay too much stress.

The horseman will realize at once that the mere offhand blocking out of the road into stages of a given number of miles each is out of the question. He must first go over the ground carefully and find the character of the roadbed, whether sandy or hard, what portions are hilly and what are level, and particularly what sort of stabling he can get, and where.

On the latter point, and on the character of the employees in charge of the horses, the smooth running of the coach is greatly dependent. Oftentimes, when the going is deep and the coach heavily loaded, the horses are called upon to extra exertion in order to make the time—a point, by the way, which is of the utmost importance if the coach is to be well done. When the tired team is taken to the stable the horses should have the best and most conscientious of care. A draughty or badly ventilated stable is therefore to be avoided as far as possible, and great pains should be taken in the selection of the horse keepers. This branch of the work will probably be productive of more annoyance than any other, for it is exceedingly difficult to secure a number of reliable men, especially where the coach is to be run for only a few weeks.

Probably there is no coachman of experience but has at some time arrived at one of his changes to find the team either absent or looking as if they had not been groomed, their harness unkempt, etc. If the men turned up at all, they were probably stupid with liquor, necessitating their immediate discharge. Such episodes show the absolute necessity of having a responsible person go over the route every day some little time after the coach, to see that the work is properly attended to. If the proprietors of the coach can not do so—which is by far the best plan—it will be necessary for them to employ a very competent head groom, who should be supplied with a smart hack or so, as a means of conveyance.

Directly horses are neglected they begin to run down, and when this happens, the running of a public coach ceases to be amusing. In a thirty-mile route there are five changes, with six horses and two men to each change; any one with experience in such matters knows that these men need looking after.

Some coachmen think it a good plan to have the head man at each change go through to the next change with his team, riding inside the coach, the object being to hold one person responsible for the care of certain horses and harness, which it is impossible to do where the horses are shifted from man to man. Others object to this arrangement on account of the extra weight to be carried; so the proper method to be pursued becomes a matter purely of individual opinion.

Now to discuss the laying out of the stages on a day's run of thirty miles and return. On the basis of one horse to the mile and six horses to each team, we find we have five teams among which to distribute the work. It may do equally well to have the teams of five horses each, thus giving us six teams; but when this is done the same stamp of horse must be used throughout, to allow of shifting into either lead or wheel. The first arrangement will generally be preferable, as it allows of an extra wheeler and leader to each four—or, in other words, allows each horse to rest one day in three.

As a general rule it will be found well to give the team at the "luncheon or middle stage," we will call it, the lightest work, and the home team the longest road, for nothing is harder on a "cold-blooded one" than to start him again soon after he has "cooled out" of a profuse sweat. In fact, if the road admits of so doing, it is a good plan to give the team on the middle stage only one long run daily, making practically only three teams on the road which run double stages, the other two doing one long stage each. It may be found necessary, on some extra sandy or hilly stage, to provide a cockhorse, and this can be made a not unattractive feature of the drive. Sometimes five miles' run over a sandy road is a good bit harder than seven over a fine one, and judgment must therefore be called into play to adjust the work properly. A stage of level macadamized road is hard on a team, because they are generally put right through without a breather; but with a few slight hills they will get considerable relief, and will travel more easily to themselves in consequence. All these points should be borne in mind in the laying out of the stages, as also in the making of the time schedule. This schedule should be made up most carefully, bearing in mind that a coach loaded with passengers is a very different vehicle from the light wagon or break, which is generally used in the preliminary drive over the road, and allowance should be made accordingly.

Ten miles an hour, including changes, is quite a good round pace when maintained for thirty miles with a heavy passenger coach, and each additional mile adds up a percentage of wear and tear on the horses far greater than an inexperienced person begins to realize. Besides this, the difficulty of maintaining such time over our average country roads day after day, in good or bad weather, is generally unappreciated by the tyro. Even the coachman who drives exceedingly well, but is without "road" experience, will do wisely to run his first coach rather under than over an average pace of ten miles an hour. It is customary to allow about five minutes for changing horses. The actual time consumed, however, should be less than this.

We will now take up the subject of the necessary horses.

This depends somewhat on the means available for the purpose. The stamp that will be found most serviceable range from fifteen one to sixteen hands high, and weigh from one thousand to eleven hundred and fifty pounds when in condition for work. They should possess a good deal of quality, for the bull-necked Western horses are mostly underbred brutes which will lie on the coachman's hands directly they are in the least leg weary. The stamp of horse that just misses being good enough for a hunter will generally answer the purpose, and should be bought for a reasonable sum. It is well to purchase horses which are nearly of a size, for in this case it is much easier to mate up the various teams satisfactorily as to temperament, etc. One often sees road teams put together on their appearance alone, regardless of temperament; this method undoubtedly gives the coachman much more practice, for it takes a good one to keep an uneven team up to its work. If Mr. Goodcoachman had the putting of such teams together, however, it is doubtful whether his lack of judgment in so doing should not outweigh his good driving from a critic's point of view. One of the greatest pleasures in the game of public coaching lies in the buying, making up, and putting together of the necessary horses. Situated as most persons are in this country, their horses must generally be purchased in the city markets, and they are in the main "green" or crudely broken. This makes it an absolute necessity to begin buying the horses not less than two months before it is intended to put the coach on the road. It is a good plan to have *all* the horses bought at least a month before the regular work begins, but they must be kept going all the time ; sorted

out and put together, so that when the coach starts
the proprietors are quite familiar with their cattle, and
everything will run smoothly. The work of breaking
in the horses will be of benefit to the coachman too,
for very few men can tool a loaded coach sixty or
seventy miles, with several changes, when they themselves are not in condition.

About three weeks before the coach is to start, the
horses should be measured for their collars, and each
horse should have his collar numbered to correspond
with his hoof brand (the number assigned to him and
branded on his hoof). This collar should be left on the
horse when he is cooling out, to avoid sore shoulders,
and should be worn together with his harness-bridle,
and bit whenever he is shifted from one stage to another. One can not dwell too urgently on the collar
question, for sore shoulders are the dread of the coachman's existence, and anything that can be done to prevent them is labor well expended. And as to the bridle
and bit, the comfort of driving a horse in the bit that
suits him is very considerable.

It will be well for the strappers to bathe each
horse's shoulder daily with a weak solution of alum
water and vinegar or a strong solution of salt and
water when the collar is removed : this contracts and
hardens the skin, and tends to prevent chafing or gall-
ing. Collars put on in the morning should remain on

all day when the horses are required to go out a second time.

The proper harness and coach are described under their respective headings, so a further description of them is superfluous. The thirty-mile route above mentioned will require six complete sets of harness—five in daily use, and the sixth at the home station in case of need. A fire or other accident might destroy a harness, when an extra set would become most useful. A really well-run route should have an extra coach, where it can be called on in case of accident to the regular. In a long route where an up and down coach is run daily it is customary to have an extra coach at each end of the line, besides one in the middle. This makes five coaches necessary to a double line of eighty or one hundred miles. These precautions may by some be considered an unnecessary extravagance; such persons will be wise not to attempt a public coach. Sooner or later they will find their coach will not come out some fine morning, and with no extra coach to fall back on temporarily they will expose themselves to ridicule. It is well to call attention to the fact that directly a man undertakes to put on a "public" he lays himself open to the criticism of "the talent," who are only too eager to find flaws in his equipment. The time schedule must be adhered to as closely as would that of a railway, and such adherence is the pride of the road coachman. If the would-be coachman says "Oh, that is all farce!" he has no conception of the part whatever. Such a man will be wise to confine himself entirely to private driving, which he can do as eccentrically as he chooses.

It is important that all the branches connected with the running of a coach be well systematized, or confusion will arise. Each groom should have his own stable tools, etc., numbered, and the same number should be placed opposite his name on the pay roll. When a groom is discharged, his successor takes his number, and so on. It is well to have the horse clothing, head collars, etc., marked with the number of the stage to which each belongs, so if a rug is accidentally misplaced it can be located at once. All such trifling details will be found to contribute largely toward a smooth working of the machinery. The person who goes over the route after the coach should keep a daily memorandum, showing by number the location of each horse on the road. If the horses are named, the index should show the number which belongs to each name, and *vice versa*. With this system, any shifting that is desired can easily be directed and accurately accomplished. It is wisest not to trust to verbal orders in such cases, but to make a signed memorandum describing what horses are to be shifted and where they are to go, for the extraordinary complications which can

occur through the medium of stupid grooms and carelessly given orders are beyond conception.

Every one who runs a public coach takes a pride
in making it come as nearly as possible to paying ex-
penses ; to do which requires a systematic, businesslike
management.

It is well to have the horses stationed a few days
before the regular work is to begin, for by driving
over the road a few times with a break the employees
can be familiarized with their duties and the time table
given somewhat of a test.

We will assume the coach to be preparing for its
first trip ; the best-looking team of the six horses at
the home end of the route is put on. The head groom
generally takes the coach from the stable to its starting place (although one of its coachmen or the guard
may do so). He wears a black melton cutaway coat
with breeches of tweed, Bedford, or whipcord and
gaiters, white stock or collar and white scarf, and
black felt top hat. The guard stands in his place on
the coach with his horn ready for use, and the two
stablemen hurry along (if the distance is great they
stand on the steps of the coach) to receive the horses
as they pull up. Each of these men carries the loin
cloths for a wheeler and a leader thrown over his
shoulder. As the coach pulls up, some ten minutes
before it is due to start, the guard jumps down and

runs to the office to receive his way bills, seat card, etc. Directly the horses stop, the grooms place the cloths quietly across their loins, slipping them carefully under the reins; off side, wheeler first, then leader; near side, leader first, then wheeler; this method allowing of one of the men being within easy reach of the leaders' heads if necessary. These men then station themselves, one at the leaders' heads, the other at the near wheeler's; the head groom dismounts, disposes of the reins and whip properly (see Chapter IX on Driving), and stands at the off wheeler's head with the coachman's driving apron across his arm.

Four or five minutes before schedule time, the guard having the ladder ready, sings out "Coach!" as a signal for the passengers to take their places. About two minutes before the time the coachman has his apron buckled, takes up his reins and whip quietly, mounts the box, compares his footboard clock with the one in the guard's pouch, and is ready to start.

This should all be done without apparent haste, but it does not look well to have to wait for a minute or so to elapse. As soon as time is up the coachman calls out "Hold fast!" "Sit tight!" or some such expression, which is repeated by the guard; the grooms strip the loin cloths off carefully, leaders first, then

wheelers, and "they are off." The guard immediately
takes his place, and in a town or city remains standing, sounding his horn as he sees the necessity for it.
Once out of town, the guard may take his seat, standing, however, when it is necessary to sound the horn.
On quiet country roads one may sometimes drive for
miles without needing the horn except to sound the
relay.

Arriving at the change, we find the team ready, as
in Plate XII, and pull up some feet beyond it. One
of the grooms holds the fresh horses while the other
jumps to unhook the off-lead trace ; he on one side
and the guard on the other quickly unhook the lead
traces, tuck the reins (which were unbuckled before
arriving) through the terrets and bridle, and pull the
leaders out of the way. They then unhook the pole
chains, leaving the hook in the kidney link ring until
they have unfastened the traces, tucked the wheel
reins, unfastened the couplings, whereupon they pull
the wheelers out of the way. A groom then takes the
fresh near wheeler, the guard the off, and slips each
into his place, putting them to as quickly as possible
(described in Chapter VIII). Meanwhile the other
groom has put the leaders in place and, if they are
sufficiently quiet, has passed the lead reins and hooked
the near lead trace ; the first groom then hooks both
inside and off-lead traces.

It is generally wise for the coachman to get down and superintend the putting to, bitting, etc, of his team, as well as to look his coach over. On a fast coach with an experienced guard, or with a jibbing team, he may remain on the box, catching the reins on his whip held vertically. He is then ready to let his team go as soon as it is put to. In the latter case he has to trust to the guard to look the coach over, etc., which is not quite consistent with first-rate coachmanship. At no time should the coachman start unless the customary warning to the passengers has been given. When sufficient assistants can be procured at a change, it is most satisfactory to have the near wheeler standing on the near side of the road (as in Plate XIII) as the coach comes up, the off wheeler on the off side abreast of him, and the leaders coupled together and standing just in front of the off wheeler. Then by pulling the coach up so that the splinter bar is about on a line with the fresh wheeler's head, the quickest kind of a change can be made.

Arriving at the end of the route, provision must be made for the necessary grooms, in case they are not carried in the coach. The guard is occupied in unloading the coach, so can not give his attention at once to the horses, which should be immediately taken out and cared for.

It will often be found well to station the horses
along the thirty-mile route as follows:

Home stable.............................. 6 horses.
First change.............................. 6   "
Second change............................ 6   "
Third change............................. 6   "
Fourth change............................ 5   "
Fifth change............................. 1   "
                                        ———
                                         30   "

This will allow the running of the horses two days
on and one day off in all the teams but the last. The
object in keeping one horse at the end of the route is
obvious, for it is never safe to put up without an extra
horse at hand. The first week or ten days, if the
travel is heavy, will tell on all the horses, but after that
with good care they will steadily improve. After a
month or so much of the amusement will be gone, for
the horses will probably know the road so well as to
need comparatively little driving.

Some of the methods advised in this chapter may
with perfect propriety be varied to suit the opinion of
an expert, but the novice will do well to experiment
thoroughly before challenging them on his own responsibility. Road coaching is like yachting, for many of
the *cognoscenti* differ in their system, while some have
no system at all. Query: Do the latter ever get to
the front? It seemed well, however, to put forward

Plate XIII : The Fast Change.

a system in this book which, although not absolute, might be of some service to the novice.

RULES FOR JUDGING PARK DRAGS AND ROAD COACHES, AS ADOPTED BY THE COACHING CLUB.

(Published by courtesy of the Club.)

THE DRAG.

THE drag should have a perch, and be less heavy than a road coach and more highly finished, with crest or monogram on the door panels or boot.

The axles may be either mail or Collinge's (not imitation).

The hind seat should be supported by curved iron braces, and be of a proper width for two grooms, without lazyback.

The lazybacks on the roof seats should be turned down when not in use.

The underside of the footboard, together with the risers,

THE COACH.

The road coach should be built stronger than a park drag, especially as to the undercarriage and axles, which latter should not measure less than two inches in diameter.

The axles may be either mail or Collinge's (not imitation).

The hind seat is usually supported by solid wooden risers with wooden curtains, but the supports may be of curved iron, as in a park drag, in which case a stationary leather curtain is used. Its seat should be wide enough for at least two beside the guard, who should occupy the near side with an extra cushion. He should have a strap to take hold of when standing to sound the horn.

The lazybacks of the box seat, hind seat, and roof seats should be stationary.

The underside of the footboard, together with the risers of

THE DRAG.

should be of the same colour as the undercarriage.

The body of the drag and the panel of the hind boot should correspond in colour.

The door of the hind boot should be hinged at the bottom, that it may be used as a table when open.

The skid and safety hook (if carried) should be hung on the off side.

It is customary to trim the outside seats in either pigskin or cloth, and the inside of the drag in morocco or cloth.

The coachman's driving apron, when not in use, should be folded on the driving cushion, outside out. Passengers' aprons, if carried, to be folded and placed on the front inside seat.

A watch and case are not essential, nor is the pocket in the driving cushion.

There should be no luggage rails or straps on the roof between the seats.

THE COACH.

the box and hind seat, should be of the same colour as the undercarriage.

The body of the coach and the panel of the hind boot should also correspond in colour.

The door of the hind boot should be hinged on the off side, to enable the guard to open it from the near hind step when the coach is in motion.

The skid and safety hook must be hung on the off side in countries in which it is customary to drive on the off side of the roadway ; for the skid should be on the outside wheel, or the coach will slide toward the ditch.

The trimming of the outside seats should be of carpet or any other suitable material, not leather. The inside of the coach is usually finished in hard wood or leather.

The coachman's driving apron, when not in use, should be folded on the driving cushion, outside out.

A footboard watch with case should be provided. The driving cushion should have a pocket on the near side.

The iron rails on the roof between the front and the back seats should have a lattice or network of leather straps to prevent small luggage, coats, rugs, etc., placed on the roof from falling off.

Inside, the drag should have :
Hat straps fastened to the roof.
Pockets on the doors. Places over the front or back seat where the lamps may be hung when not in use. An extra jointed whip.

The umbrella basket, when carried, to be hung on the near side.

Inside, the coach should have :
Hat straps fastened to the roof. Leather pockets at the sides or on the doors. An extra jointed whip.

The basket should be hung on the near side and in front of the guard's seat. The horn should be placed in the basket with its mouthpiece up.

Lamps off. Lamps inside coach.

Side lamps in place and ready for use.

Two extra lead bars, consisting of a main and side bar, fastened to the back of the hind seat with straps. Main bar above.

Lead bars put on with screw heads of furniture up.

The following articles to be neatly stowed inside the front boot : A small kit of tools. An extra lead and wheel trace. A rein splicer or two double buckles of different sizes. Extra hame straps. Loin cloths for team and the necessary waterproof aprons should be carried in a convenient and accessible part of the drag.

Two extra lead bars, consisting of a main and side bar, fastened to the back ot the hind seat with straps. Main bar above.

Lead bars put on with screw heads of furniture up.

The following articles to be neatly stowed in a convenient part of the coach : A wheel jack. A chain trace. Extra hame straps, Extra lead trace. A bearing rein. A rein splicer (a short strap of the same width as the reins, with a buckle at either end) or two double buckles of different sizes. A kit of tools, comprising a wrench, hammer, coil of wire, punch, hoofpick, and a knife. Two extra large rings for kidney

THE DRAG.

It is usual for a park drag to be fitted with luncheon boxes, wine racks, etc. ; also a box on the roof called an " imperial." This latter is never carried except when going to the races or a luncheon.

THE COACH.

links or a pair of pole pieces. An extra bit.

The guard should be appropriately dressed, and should have a way-bill pouch with a watch fitted on one side, and a place provided for the key of the hind boot.

PARK HARNESS.

Pole chains should be burnished and have spring hooks. The chains should be of a length which will permit of snapping both hooks into the pole ring. If too short, one end should be hooked in the pole-head ring and the other in a link. If too long, one end should be snapped in the pole-head ring, and the other brought through said ring (from the outside in) and snapped in a link.

Cruppers with buckles on all horses.*

Loin straps and trace bearers are permissible.

ROAD HARNESS.

Pole chains should be burnished or black, but pole head and chains should be alike. Hooks should have India-rubber rings, not spring hooks. Chains with single hooks should be put on pole head from inside out, then passed through the kidney link and hooked into one of the links of the chain.

Cruppers with or without buckles on wheelers, but not necessarily on leaders, unless bearing reins are used. Martingale back strap. Trace bearers on the leaders from the hames to tug buckles are permissible.

No loin straps.

---

* While cruppers with buckles are perfectly proper, it seems unwise to make them compulsory. Many experienced amateurs are opposed to the use of buckles on the cruppers of any park harness, and in the author's opinion justifiably so.

PARK HARNESS.

Face pieces (drops).

Martingales around the collars of wheelers, and not through the kidney links alone.

Martingales on all horses.

No rings on coupling reins.

Mountings of coach and harness and the buttons on servants' liveries should be of the same metal.

Wheel traces with metal loop ends, not chains.

Wheelers' inside traces shorter than outside traces, unless the inside roller bolt is enlarged to give the same result.

Lead traces straight or lapped, not crossed.

Eyes on end of hames through which the kidney links pass.

Plain kidney links. No kidney-link rings on leaders.

Solid draught eyes on hames.

Clip inside of trace leather, and showing rivet heads only.

Full-bearing reins with bit and bridoon. Buxton bits preferred.

Single point strap to tug buckle.

Metal or ribbon fronts to bridles. If ribbon, the colour should match the livery waistcoat.

The crest or monogram should be on the rosettes, face pieces, winkers, pads, and martingale flaps.

ROAD HARNESS.

Face pieces (optional).

Martingales around the collars, and not through the kidney links alone.

No martingales on leaders; kidney-link rings on leaders.

Mountings, preferably of brass, but at least all of the same metal throughout.

Wheel traces with French loop or chain ends. Chain put on roller bolt with chain out and ring in.

Wheelers' inside traces shorter than outside traces, unless the inside roller bolt is enlarged to give the same result.

Lead traces lapped, crossed, or straight.

Hook ends to hames.

Chain and short kidney links or all chain.

Ring draught eyes on hames.

One or more bearing reins are optional.

Metal or leather fronts to bridle. If leather, the colour to match the coach.

A crest or monogram is not generally used in road work, but instead lead bars or a special device

PARK HARNESS.

Ribbon or coloured rosettes are inappropriate.

Hames straps put on with points inside—i. e., to the off side on the near horse and the near side on the off horse. .

Reins of single brown leather.

Draught reins sewed in one piece, with end buckles only.

Lead traces with screw heads of the cockeyes up.

All parts of the harness should be double, and neatly stitched.

Collars to be of black patent leather shaped to the neck.

The hames bent to fit the collar accurately.

Harness black. All straps should be of proper length, but not too short.

When the owner or his representative drives, the stable shutters should be down; otherwise up.

ROAD HARNESS.

in brass is put on the winkers and rosettes.

Hames straps put on with points inside—i. e., to the off side on the near horse and the near side on the off horse.

Reins of single brown leather.

Draught reins sewed in one piece, with end buckles only.

Traces with screw heads of the cockeyes and chain ends up.

All straps preferably of single leather.

Collars may be of patent, plain black, or brown leather; straight, thick, and full padded.

The hames straight to fit the collar.

Harness black or brown.

SOME COACH-HORN CALLS.

THE START.

OFF SIDE.

CHAPTER IV.

WHILE the term four-in-hand is very properly embraced under the title of the preceding chapter, Coaching, the latter term is not applicable to four-in-hand driving at large, and the two should not be confused. The word coaching applies only to the sport when a coach or drag is the vehicle used. Four-in-hand work embraces the remainder of the field.

It is almost imperative for every coaching man to have some vehicle besides his coach to which he can drive four horses, as the coach is often too heavy for exercising, etc.

Four-in-hand driving is a delightful sport in itself, and although it can scarcely be brought to the acme of perfection in detail of which coaching admits, nevertheless it is not to be despised.

It is necessary that every man who goes into coaching shall have passed through the school of four-in-hand driving. In Plates XIV and XV are shown the body break, with and without perch. These two carriages may be considered the standard four-in-hand

Plate XV : Body Break without Perch.

Plate XVII : Char à banc.

Plate XVIII: Skeleton Break.

traps; and while there are several other carriages, such as the roof seat break (Plate XVI), the omnibus (Plate XCVIII), the French *char à banc* (Plate XVII), and the skeleton break (Plate XVIII), which are perfectly practical for the driving of four horses, they can not, nevertheless, be considered as in the best of form. Of course, in the case of the omnibus we have a carriage which is useful for other purposes as well, and often answers for the man who has not the time or the means to indulge in a vehicle which is adapted to four-in-hand work alone. It may be wise, however, to advise against the use of hybrid vehicles for four-in-hand work on general principles, as in most cases their cost is about the same as that of the standard carriages, and they have ordinarily very little in themselves to warrant a deviation in their favour. Breaks and four-in-hand traps generally should be considered as sporting vehicles, and treated in their appointment on that basis. Stable liveries should be used, also road harness with the sporting type of bits, etc. Custom has, perhaps, made it admissible that at times the servants may wear full liveries on a break which has a hind seat similarly arranged to that of a coach; but it should be remembered primarily that such carriages are classified under the term hybrid, and are therefore scarcely to be considered as within the pale of criticism. It can invariably be said to be in far better

taste to turn them out in the more simple style which
conforms to the undress livery ; and the adherence to
the pot hat and mufti on the part of their owner is
on all occasions advisable.

In Plate XIX is shown the arrangement of the
bars, etc., for the "putting to" of six horses. While
the driving of six is not considered as in the best of
form, there are times when it will be found useful, and
for this reason the photograph has been introduced.

Plate XIX : Arrangement of Poles and Bars
for Six Horses.

Plate XX : Cocking Cart.

CHAPTER V.

TANDEM driving is a most delightful sport, and productive of a great deal of skill on the part of the man who practices it constantly and with a variety of horses. It seems to be somewhat of a fad with coaching and four-in-hand men generally to affect to despise a tandem as beneath their dignity. Such an affectation is absurd, for tandem driving requires the consideration of many points which do not exist in the driving of four; and although the latter sport demands more finished horsemanship as a whole, tandem driving furnishes a field for practice, and the use of hands and whip, which are most valuable to a coachman.

When one has, for example, two highly strung horses with sensitive mouths which are new to tandem work, he has really one of the prettiest opportunities for the display of finished horsemanship and hands, if he would bring these horses to their work properly without the constant assistance of his groom.

Probably every tandem driver has seen a leader fall over backward, and realized that the performance was

in nine cases out of ten due to the bad hands of the
driver. Horses of the disposition above described require a constant and delicate feeling of the bit. When
such is not the practice, and the opportunity is furnished by a sufficiently loose rein, they will rush forward, and naturally, coming suddenly against the bit
held with the vicelike grip of a heavy-handed whip,
are apt to jib and plunge.

It is at times more or less of an impossibility to
avoid the leader's coming back suddenly, thus leaving
a certain amount of slack rein, and in such cases skilful
handling shows to the best advantage. The skilled
hand will drop itself naturally, catching the rush with
a slight pressure at the outset, which is gradually
increased to one more severe until the horse faces
his bit.

On the average level road or slight down grade the
leader is not expected to do any work, and must be
gently restrained so that his traces hang possibly a
foot below their level when extended. The leader
should never be allowed to pull the wheeler along, as it
is a most dangerous performance, which eight wheelers
out of ten will resent by either jibbing or coming down
on their knees.

The driving of tandem was practically originated by
a custom on the part of some of the sportsmen in the
hunting countries of taking their hunter to cover as a

leader, this method being the nearest approach to having him led out. They of course did not allow him to do any work, and he simply jogged along comfortably to himself until the meet was reached. The custom of driving in this manner gradually grew into favour, and became more or less a sport of itself. Within the past few years it has been taken up somewhat by ladies. Lady Georgiana Curzon has written quite an interesting little chapter in the Badminton Driving on the subject, and I take the liberty of quoting her description of the arrangement and dimensions of the bars as she uses them, for they are especially appropriate to ladies' driving, and make rather a nice distinction between the two types. "This method involves the use of two bars, the first twenty-nine and one half inches long, and the second twenty-three inches long ; the first one has at each end twenty-two inches of trace, which hook on to the tugs of the wheeler's traces ; in the centre of this bar is a small chain ten and one half inches long, which fastens on to the wheeler's collar by the ordinary kidney link and ring as for a pole chain. This is to prevent the bars touching the wheeler when standing still. In front of the main bar is a large hook, on to which is affixed the second bar, the space between the two being four and one half inches. To the second bar are hooked the leader's traces."

Tandem carts or gigs are made with straight or very slightly bent shafts, which should hang nearly level when harnessed, although a trifling inclination towards the tail is admissible. A cart should never hang "by the head."

It will readily be seen by these suggestions that the height of the cart is a very considerable factor in the selection of the wheeler. The arrangement and buckling of the tugs is a most important point, for on this the ease of motion of the cart depends in a very great measure. When the shafts are level and the buckles dropped or raised to suit this condition, the tug bellyband is buckled loosely; it should have plenty of freedom to allow of an upward and downward play of the shafts when the cart is driven over an uneven surface. The practice of buckling it tight has made many a novice decide that he does not care to have his digestion upset by the jolting of a tandem cart, whereas, if the cart is well balanced and properly harnessed, it is a most delightful vehicle to drive.

A harness which is thoroughly tandem is shown in Plate XXXIV, but there has been a tendency of late years to introduce the park refinements by lining, double leather, etc., so that style also must be in a measure considered. The livery of the groom is shown in Plates XXXVII, XXXVIII, and XL; but for road use in the country, with the true tandem harness, stable clothes are most suitable.

It may be well to state that the groom, when left alone to hold a tandem, should stand on the off side of the wheeler's head, so that, if necessary, he can use his left hand to hold the wheeler and his right to grasp the leader's reins. (The same method should be adopted when one man is left to hold a four.) When the owner is up, he should stand in front of and facing the leader, and either holding both reins lightly or standing with arms folded some few feet distant.

When the owner is driving without a passenger, the tailboard of the cart should be up, and his servant should sit beside him. The cocking cart, however, savours so much of a four-wheeler in its arrangement that the servant should always be carried on the hind seat or rumble. The lamps on any tandem cart should be removed in the daytime, unless they are provided with shutters or can be turned in the irons so as to show only a plain black surface.

The carts given here are those which have been adopted as standard by the Tandem Club of New York, and are in the main copies of old prints.

The cocking cart (Plate XX) is taken from the print by Newhouse entitled Going to the Moors. It is a cumbersome vehicle and should only be used in a very large stable, as it is scarcely suitable for everyday and all-around service.

The Whitechapel cart (Plate XXI) has been in use for many years and is of good standard pattern; it is a smart and practical vehicle, but the greatest care must be exercised in the harnessing of it, to prevent its looking too much "down by the tail."

The going-to-cover cart (Plate XXII) is taken from Henderson's print of that title, and, by the way, no more truly sporting picture of the tandem is extant. The horses are both of a rattling, breedy stamp, and no better ideal can be found at the present time.

The spicy team cart (Plate XXIII) is somewhat after that in Walsh's print of that name, and has considerable character.

The tandem gig (Plate XXIV) is taken from Alken's print of A Sporting Tandem, and is a very good pattern of a tandem vehicle to carry two.

There is no carriage which requires more severity of treatment than the dogcart. It will be noticed that in all the examples shown here the iron work, etc., is as plain and simple as possible.

A basket should never be carried, except possibly for road work; and as to a horn, it is probably better form in this country to dispense with it entirely.

Plate XXI: Whitechapel Cart.

Plate XXII : " Going-to-Cover " Cart.

Plate XXIII: "Spicy Team" Cart.

Plate XXIV : Tandem Gig.

There are a few four-wheeled vehicles which are appropriate for tandem use, as, for example, the shooting drag or Scotch phaëton, as shown in Nimrod's Life of a Sportsman, and the four-wheeled dogcart shown in Henderson's print entitled Late for the Mail. (See Plate LXVIII.)

CHAPTER VI.

THE intention of this book is to treat more particularly the appointment of our modern vehicles, and to point out the general details which are necessary to a finished equipage; but a few words on the subject of the horse may not be out of place.

The numerous horse shows which have sprung into existence within the past few years have aroused a general interest in horsey matters. Even the casual observer must have noticed the marked improvement in the harness classes at our recent shows, and to those who are interested the improvement seems little short of marvellous.

When the National Horse Show Association's first show was held, in 1883, many of the exhibitors entered their horses in classes to which they were unsuited. For this reason the judges were often obliged to pass over a good horse, and in consequence were unfairly criticised by the spectators, many of whom could not appreciate the why and wherefore. By degrees a more general understanding of the requirements has been arrived at, and a marked improvement is the result.

The introduction of cable and electric tramways has thrown an enormous number of cheap horses on our market, and, in consequence, even the better class of horse will not bring his value, although the "rare good one" has never commanded higher figures than at the present time. This temporary depression is bound to improve the quality of the horses bred in this country, for the following reason:

Throughout the West a certain class of farmers have been marketing hundreds of monstrosities masqueraded as horses, which should never have been seen outside of a dime museum. The enormous demand for street-car horses encouraged these breeders in the purchasing of broken-down, unsound mares. These mares they bred to slab-sided trotting stallions and grade percherons, and, sad to say, their produce was readily sold. As soon as this class of farmer finds an absence of demand for his production he will try a crop more in his line. This will leave the field clear for the farmer who breeds carefully and intelligently, for there always will be a good market for high-grade horses.

The better the horse the higher price he will

bring. In consequence of this, great care will be taken in the selection of sires, and none but high-class mares will be used in the stud, for the produce of inferior ones will not be worth stable room.

What more appropriate time, therefore, could be found for the institution of standards of type than the present, and what organization is better fitted to assume this responsibility than the National Horse Show Association of America? Not only the driving public, but the breeders themselves, would be benefited by such a move. The latter would then be enabled to breed with some definite object in view, and not at random, as most of them do now.

It is a well-known fact in breeding, that by selection one can in a few generations so accentuate a peculiarity as to make it a deformity, or *vice versa.*

The pigeon, owing to the rapidity with which it reproduces, furnishes the best illustration of the extraordinary results which selection can effect. From the common blue rock have been evolved the tumblers, pouters, fantails, jacobins, and even the now famous homing pigeons.

Any one who has made a study of the breeding of cattle, dogs, pigs, sheep, chickens, etc., knows the importance of proper selection and its possibilities.

This only goes to show what is possible in the breeding of horses, though the process of evolution is necessarily slower.

The standards of type should be made, to some extent, for the breeder to " grow to." In other words, we must not be satisfied with existing specimens, but from them portray even more perfect ideals without attempting impossibilities.

The breeding of trotters for speed alone has been an injury to the horses of this country. The men who do this generally throw from twenty to thirty useless runts on the market to each fast horse they produce. While we are undoubtedly patriotic enough to appreciate the surprising results which have been effected, we doubt whether they are beneficial to the horse world at large.

Fortunately, many trotting-horse breeders are beginning to realize that it pays better to add size, conformation, and uniformity to their requirements, for they are thus enabled to get good prices for their culls as roadsters, etc.

Certain lines of trotting blood are producing individuals peculiarly adapted to the spider phaëton, light gig, etc. When the breeders fully appreciate the value of such horses they will breed with a view to reproducing and improving the good types.

The old Morgan trotter is probably the nearest

suited to the requirements of the brougham or carriage horse of any strain produced in America. Unfortunately, this blood is almost extinct, but there is no reason why it can not be revived in the course of time.

What one might term the "fancy carriage horse" is a comparatively new type in this country. Those we have are for the most part mere freaks, and bred on no particular lines.

There is nothing like blood, and there is no blood like that of the English thoroughbred, because of its long establishment. It is a curious fact that as early as the fourteenth century Henry VIII issued an edict prohibiting his subjects from using any stallion under fourteen hands high for breeding purposes, and yet many would have us think that all the good qualities of the English thoroughbred came from the horses of Eastern countries. It is quite certain that racing existed in England more than fifty years before the importation of any Arab, Barb, or Turkish blood.

Now a trotting thoroughbred was the progenitor of our American trotter, and careful selection has established the present breed.

The heavyweight thoroughbred hunter has been produced in the same manner, as has also the thoroughbred polo pony, two extreme types. We find occasional examples of high action in the thorough-bred, and they are quite frequent in the trotter.

Let such horses as these be selected as sires for our carriage horses. The more they vary in type the better, provided the proper mares can be found to breed to them.

The author is thoroughly convinced that an intelligent commingling of the blood of the thoroughbred with that of the American trotter will enable us to supply all the types necessary for heavy harness purposes, and this combination will retain that much-to-be-desired element, quality.

The English hackney is by no means to be despised, but it is probable that the combination just mentioned will produce a horse even better adapted to our uses.

We have benefited enormously by the English thoroughbred; let us try to show our cousins across the sea that we have not hidden our talent in the ground, but have produced an animal superior to the hackney in its own sphere of usefulness.

It is doubtful if we can at present equal the superb exhibition which a high-class hackney makes when shown to hand. The coarseness about the throat and shortness of the neck, which to a great extent prevail in the breed, do not show as much in this case as when in harness, especially when the customary side reins are used.

The hackney is a capital type of an old gentleman's park hack, is exceedingly well suited to a lady's phaëton or small two-wheeler, and its pony types are very good.

Prejudice should not stand in the way of our benefiting, where possible, by the introduction of this blood. Let us try the effect of crossing them intelligently on our trotters or with thoroughbreds. Let this progeny compete with true American-bred ones, and may the *best horse win.*

The requirements for our future ideals will be much on the following lines:

Conformation, quality, suitable size and type (described); weight (described); pace (described); action (style of, described); colour and soundness. With requirements of this sort, in which the descriptions are carefully thought out, one could form quite a close idea of what is wanted in any particular class. These requirements could be numbered, and in various classes they could be referred to under their number for the sake of simplification.

Oftentimes a fine large pair of horses will look well before a full-sized landau, while before a brougham they would look out of proportion, and thereby detract greatly from the general effect. With require-

Plate XXV : Sensational Goer in Action.

Plate XXVI: A Brilliant Pair.

ments giving the necessary weight and height, the entry of these horses in their proper class would be assured. It is well for every horse owner to bear in mind that because his horse happens to be a good one, he is not necessarily suited to any and every variety of vehicle.

CHAPTER VII.

COACHMEN.

UNDER this head may be said to come the amateur coachman, professional coachman, and body or private coachman. "The amateur coachman" is a term known to all. The so-called "professional coachman" is one who, having graduated from the lower schools, makes a business of breaking in horses to the nicer harness work and of instructing in driving, etc. (this term may be equally well applied to head coachmen generally).

The body or private head coachman is the one with whom we have first to deal, and it is doubtful if there are twenty-five men in America to-day to whom the term can be rightly applied.

There are, of course, a great many men who consider themselves coachmen who, though they may be qualified to fill the positions they occupy, have not had the opportunities of learning the nice points of their profession. These men should be considered as undercoachmen, and not confused with the finished masters of their art.

Most of the so-called coachmen in this country have been merely strappers in their stables at home, and, having launched themselves in a strange land under the sobriquet of "coachmen," have readily found places in the service of employers who were not over-well informed, and often at wages which none but experienced men should command.

A head coachman becomes such after years of hard training under a master (either professional or amateur) who is thoroughly posted, and then only when he possesses a suitable temperament, hands, receptive faculties, application, and appearance, together with the ability to manage men and the education necessary to the keeping of his accounts, etc. While, of course, those needing a servant so well qualified as a head coachman should be are not numerous, they are sufficiently so to warrant a sketch of some of the training which such a man must undergo.

Beginning in his boyhood as exerciser, and later as a breaker of colts to saddle, he goes through a hard and somewhat rough school, his instructor probably being considerable of a martinet. Then, selected from among several others of his kind, he is advanced to the harness stable, where for some time he is made generally useful and is familiarized with the minor details of stable duties; he is taught how to walk smartly, and not with the slouchy step of the plowboy, and how to put a certain snap into his way of doing his work. By degrees, as a strapper, the cleaning of horses, harness, carriages, saddles, bridles, leathers, and all the incidental and additional duties are mastered, and he commences his career as a groom in livery. In this capacity he has to learn a great many little niceties as to the proper way of filling the positions of tiger, carriage, and pad groom. These qualifications mastered, he is passed to the degree of undercoach-man, and then, if he is to be further advanced, he must be sufficiently interested in his work to learn the practical care of the horse; his feeding, treat-ment, etc., in case of sudden sickness (and before a veterinarian can be summoned); he must look into horseshoeing from an intelligent standpoint, so that he can advise with the farrier as to the correction of some defect in balance or in action; he must be well posted in mouthing and bitting as applied to horses of different temperaments; he must know how to harness his horses properly, and how to drive a single horse, a pair, a tandem, or a four, in a fin-ished and workmanlike manner, and, finally, he must not use liquor to excess. How true the maxim is, that "a coachman is born, not made"; for, with all the requisite making here outlined, the number of men with the keenness and ability to profit by such training is extremely small.

Probably after reading this description most persons will say: "That is all very well, but it is too idealistic for me. I don't believe such a paragon exists."

That he does exist in America is, however, a fact, although in only about a one-per-cent ratio; and it is in justice to such men that some discrimination should be made in the use of the word "coachman." Possibly twenty-four per cent of our so-called coachmen are really deserving of the title "under-coachman," and only need the opportunities to qualify them for a higher sphere, but it is doubtful if the remaining seventy-five per cent will ever get beyond the stage of harnessing one or a pair in a happy-go-lucky way, hauling it or them around to do their employer's bidding, and feeding each nag four quarts of oats three times a day, with bran mash on Saturdays. Such men can only be called "farmers" or "cowmilkers."

Those who do not wish to keep an elaborate but a well-equipped establishment, must therefore draw from the above-mentioned twenty-four per cent; but they must also understand that the men who will accept small places generally do so because they have not the necessary qualifications to warrant their filling more experienced ones.

It is often a wise plan for an amateur of means,

who wishes to work to the top of the ladder himself, to employ a smart, keen man of this type, for, though together they may make mistakes, the pleasure of acquiring knowledge of one's own experience is sufficient compensation.

It is a curious fact that many of the men employed as coachmen have not the faintest conception of what the word means in its full sense. For example, no good coachman, amateur or professional, *will ever* lounge on his box, and nothing will show a man's ignorance sooner than such behaviour. A well-trained and self-respecting servant will never smoke on one of his employer's vehicles when in livery (either stable or dress).

All these little things go to show the stamp of the man; and though many err simply through ignorance of the proprieties and with no intention of being insolent (which is the only term for either of the performances above mentioned), the fact of their so doing shows at once the amount of training they have had. So it is right through the list, for in numberless little ways the gold can be distinguished from the dross, and almost at first glance.

CHAPTER VIII.

THERE are many nice distinctions which go toward making a harness effective and appropriate to its purpose.

In heavy harness such a trifle as the shape of a buckle gives character to the whole. The horseshoe buckle, for example, should properly be used on all harnesses which are intended purely for sporting driving—namely, the tandem, four-in-hand road, dogcart, exercising gig, etc. This class of harness is made of single leather throughout, or of double leather plainly stitched; it is furnished with what is called a ring draught on the hames, and requires the use of suitable bits—namely, the plain or ring snaffle, elbow cheek, Hanoverian Pelham, or Liverpool. The collars are straight and much more heavily padded than those for dress use. They may be either plain black, patent, or brown leather, or patent leather with brown leather fronts.

Having mentioned the sporting bits, it may be well to state that a Buxton or gig bit with bridoon in a harness, calls for a nonsporting treatment and the highest class of finish throughout.

At the end of the chapter on Coaching will be found rules as adopted by the Coaching Club (of New York), which include a definition of the proper harness for the park and road four.

The difference between harness for heavy work and that adapted to the light trotting or road wagon is most marked, while each is equally a work of art in its way. A few harnesses of the heavy type are illustrated and described as follows:

THE RUNABOUT HARNESS (PLATE XXVII).

This harness is suited to any light nondescript two or four wheeler.

The pad is not as heavy as in the brougham, dog-cart, or gig.

The English tug which is shown is, of course, used with a shaft stop, enabling one to dispense with a breeching.

It is intended that the tug girth shall lie quite snug. A plain English bridle with square blinkers looks the tidiest for the work, and almost any of the sporting styles of bit may be used.

The collar is generally made fairly light and straight with plain draught hames, but a shaped

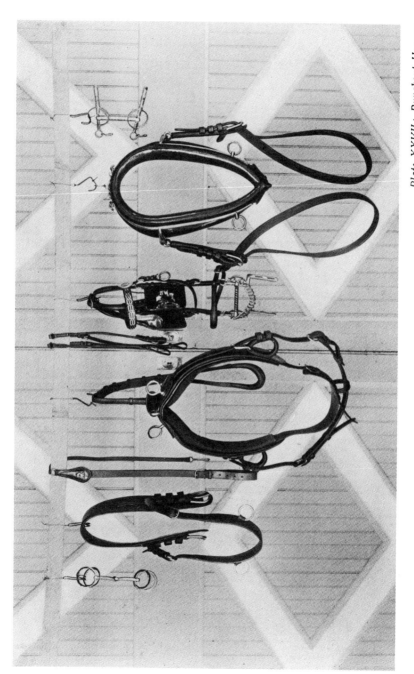

Plate XXVII : Runabout Harness.

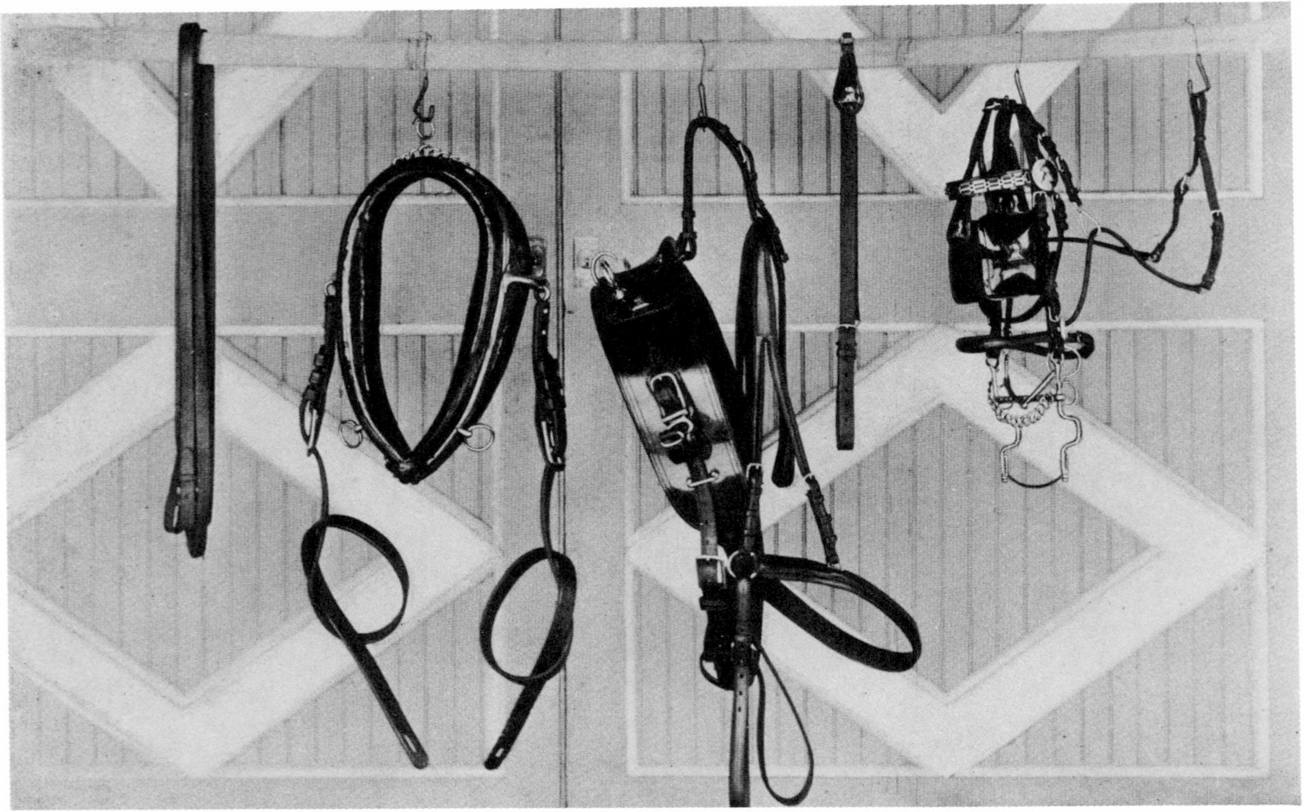

Plate XXVIII: Single Brougham Harness.

collar with plain draughts is not improper in a run-about which is smartly turned out for town use.

The single bearing rein is used with this harness, which comes properly under the "semi-sporting" head.

THE SINGLE BROUGHAM HARNESS (PLATE XXVIII).

We notice first the Buxton bit in the bridle. This bit indicates immediately the dressy character of the harness. We find a neat, fair-sized pad with French loop tugs, so made that the shaft is kept close to the horse's side.

The collar is shaped and the hames have plain draught eyes.

The standing martingale is the correct one. It will be seen that this harness is of lined leather throughout, and the buckles, etc., are of a nonsporting shape.

The breeching, which is of graceful construction, is supported by two straps which meet about two thirds of the way up, but *do not* form a wide expanse on which to put a crest or monogram. The bridle front is one of the most refined in style, and is in keeping with the full bearing rein, etc. Either square or horseshoe blinkers are proper.

THE GIG HARNESS.

The difference between this and the brougham harness is slight, but still there is a difference, and though the two harnesses are to a great extent similar, there are some trifling points which make each appropriate to its own use.

The breeching is replaced by the kicking strap, which may be used or dispensed with at pleasure.

The gig bit with plain bridoon and short bearing rein is a trifle the more proper; but the Buxton bit and full bearing rein may be used.

These trifling points are brought out, not arbitrarily, but in order to show the nice details which go toward making a successful whole.

THE SINGLE VICTORIA HARNESS (Plate XXIX).

Here we come to the most refined of the refined, to the most dressy of the dressy, and, in fact, to a harness which should never be used except on irreproachable horseflesh, and then only when the general appointments are in keeping.

A close observer will notice all the nice points in which this harness differs from its predecessors, particularly as to the shape of the pad and blinkers.

The horse to carry such a harness must have

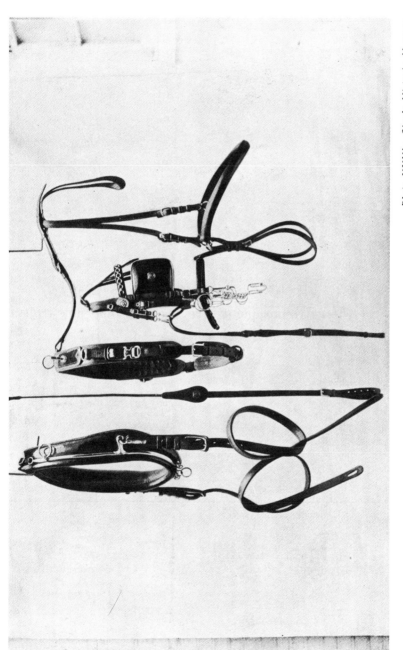

Plate XXIX : Single Victoria Harness.

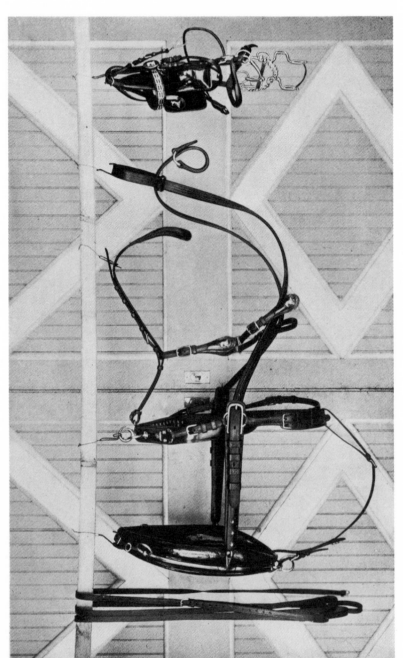

Plate XXX : Pair-horse Brougham Harness.

quality—it can easily be seen how absurd it would look on a coarse one—and he must also be a brilliant goer. The servant must be spruceness itself, of medium height, and slim. The carriage must be on *graceful* lines and painted as inconspicuously as possible. This harness can also be used on a smart lady's phaëton.

THE PAIR-HORSE BROUGHAM HARNESS, FOR OFF HORSE
(PLATE XXX); ALSO
FOUR-HORSE PARK HARNESS LEAD AND WHEEL, NEAR
SIDE (PLATE XXXI).

This pair-horse brougham harness, belonging as it does to the more dressy class, demands the Buxton or gig bit, together with the full bearing rein and bridoon; the plain kidney link and plain draught; loin straps and lining throughout, etc. The billets or loops which guard the trace ends should never be of metal, but may be made in one piece.

Twisted metal for the hames, terrets, buckles, etc., is *very bad form in any harness.*

The brougham harness here shown differs very slightly in appearance from the wheel set of a four-in-hand park harness, shown in Plate XXXI. The use of loin straps on the latter is a somewhat disputed point, but with the full bearing rein, etc., they are undoubtedly correct, while not nearly as attractive.

The park wheel harness has a pad terret similar to the one shown in the road four-in-hand harness. The wheeler's bridle has overhead rings, besides which the outside drop on the throat latch is made double to allow of the rendering of the reins without interference with the bearing rein; sometimes the lower ring has a revolving bar through the centre to make the reins run more freely. Such details, however, are purely matters of fancy on the part of the coachman himself.

FOUR-IN-HAND ROAD HARNESS (PLATES XXXII AND XXXIII).

The bits, being so clearly shown in the photograph, we will consider as an illustration of the type, and will proceed at once to a discussion of the difference between this harness and that for park use, taking each point in order.

The bridle is made for full (or long) bearing reins in the park, for short bearing reins in the road (often dispensed with altogether in the latter).

The bits are "dress" *versus* "sporting." The bridle fronts quiet in park, bold in road. No face pieces in road. The other parts require a somewhat more explanatory treatment.

The park hames have full kidney links which open with a hinge at the top. These openings enable one

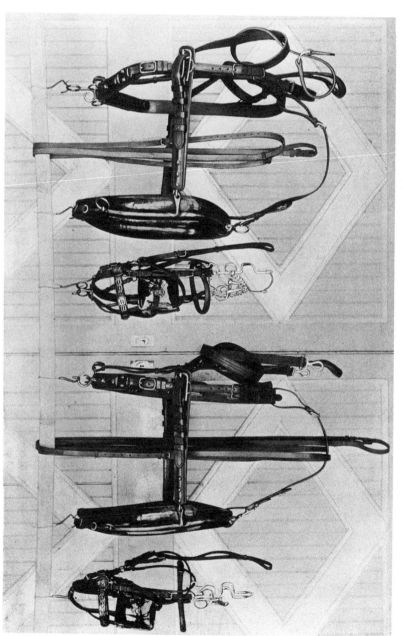

Plate XXXI: Lead and Wheel
Park Four-in-Hand Harness

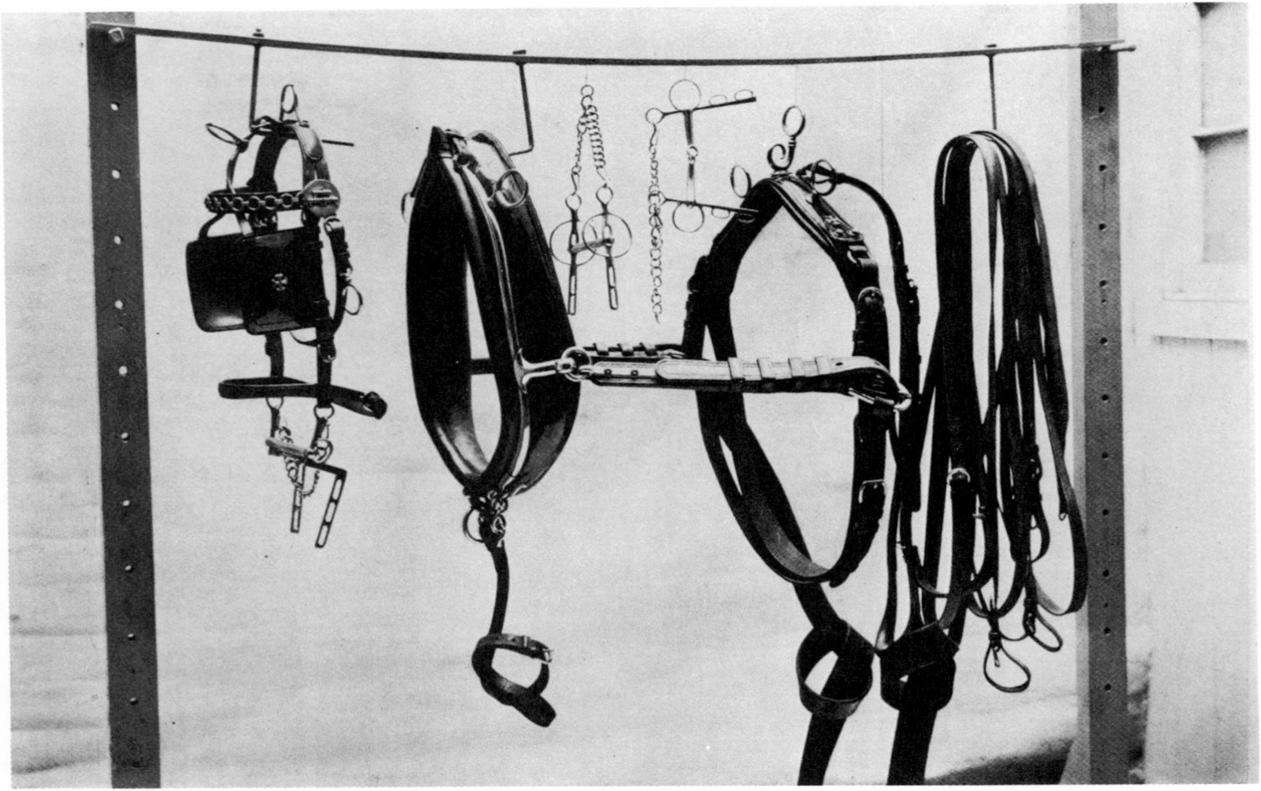

Plate XXXII : Four-in-Hand

to pass the link through the *eyes* on the *ends* of the *hames*.

The road harness has a short link with a chain attached to it. This link is passed through the eye which is on the end of the inner part of the hames, and the chain is hooked over the hook which is on their outer part. This arrangement enables one to fit the hames to collars differing widely in size with greater expedition.

In the park wheel harness *generally,* and in the road wheel harness *always,* the point of the martingale should be of sufficient length to allow of its going completely around the collar, thereby guarding against the slipping of the hames. The ring draught is better suited to road work, and is less liable to cause sore shoulders. Oftentimes in a road harness the trace itself is stitched into the ring instead of being fastened by a clip, but this method is more clumsy.

Quite a noticeable difference between the two harnesses lies in the tug straps. In the park harness the trace buckle has a small extra eye top and bottom, into which the " Newmarket " tug and guide straps are *stitched* (they are sometimes stitched into the buckle itself). The eye in the upper part of the trace buckle carries a short strap with a buckle end, into which the point of a strap stitched to the pad is fastened. This makes a somewhat neater finish than the full strap used in road work.

The latter is simply a plain straight strap made with one or two billets or loops to keep it in place. The point is passed through the upper side of the trace buckle from outside in, then through the ring on the pad from inside out, and back to its own buckle, thus bringing the point down. Practically the only remaining difference, beyond the general distinctions between dress and road harness, previously described, lies in the trace ends. The park traces have square metal ends, and the road traces have either stitched loops (called French loops) or chain ends. The loops are more practical for quick changing.

TANDEM HARNESS (PLATE XXXIV).

The accompanying photograph portrays an excellent example of a tandem harness in the accepted sense of the word.

The tandem is a purely sporting equipage, and is really not suited to park work, pure and simple. However, as the tendency during the past few years seems to have been toward the separation of the tandem into road and park types, it may be as well to state that the harness here shown will come under the head of "Suitable for the Road."

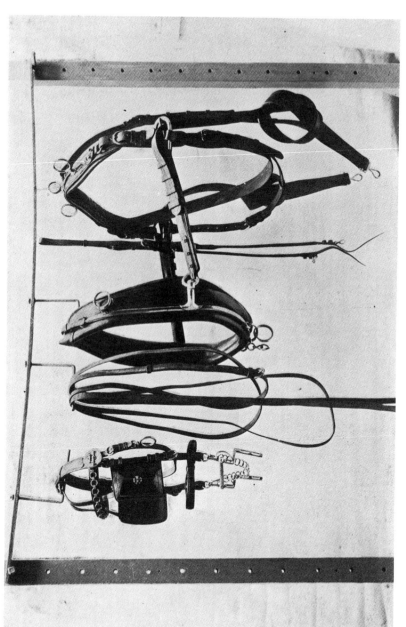

Plate XXXIII: Four-in-Hand
Road Harness (Lead).

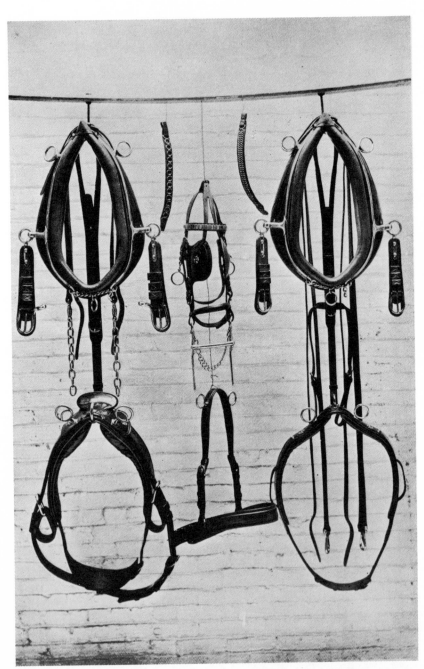

Plate XXXIV: Tandem Harness.

The park harness would presumably be evolved on the Buxton and gig bit system as previously described. In other words, the general refinements which accompany these bits would be applied.

It is almost unnecessary to go into the various details in descriptive form, for the illustration is exceedingly clear. It may be well, however, to call attention to the breast collar, which hangs in the centre beneath the bridle.

This looks very sporting for the road leader of a breedy stamp, with a good shoulder and long, clean-cut neck. The old print Going to Cover, which is probably one of the best illustrations of a tandem, shows this collar in use with good effect.

The hame collars shown in the photograph are of patent leather with brown leather fronts. This is not a necessity, but is rather a smart characteristic. To correspond with the collars, the pad is what is called "basil-faced"; in other words, it has a narrow rim of brown leather showing beyond the patent leather in both front and rear.

Two or three bridle fronts are shown, any of which may be used according to individual taste.

The elbow cheek bit is probably the most correct of any for this purpose, and the shape of the blinkers in the photograph is a trifle better adapted to tandem work than any other.

It will be noticed that this harness has ring draught hames, together with horseshoe buckles. The hames themselves are made mainly of brass, but the hooks at the throat of the collar, the shoulders which carry the rings, together with the rings themselves, are of steel, which must be kept burnished. The eyes on the wheeler's trace buckles, into which the leader's traces are snapped, are also of steel.

POLE CHAINS *VERSUS* POLE PIECES.

This point seems to be very little understood in this country. The pole chain is for use on carriages intended for their owners' driving alone. They should not be used on any carriage to be driven by a servant. The proper chain for sporting work is a plain single oval link with a single snap hook at either end, or with a ring or delta in one end and a snap hook in the other. The links in chains intended for purely park driving are made a little more square in shape, and have a single snap hook in each end. Twisted or double chains or double snap hooks should never be used; the latter allow of the dropping of two or three links—a most reprehensible practice, hence the "clanking pole chains."

Many owners of private stables are so occupied as to be unable to give them the necessary supervision or attention, and in consequence the management of all the details must be left to servants.

Those who have sufficient leisure will find occupation for many pleasant hours in "fussing" about their stables, considering whether the harness appears to the best advantage when hung this way or that, whether this or that horse's tail is properly trimmed, whether the shoeing has been attended to, and so on.

A man who drives tandem or four-in-hand should take down his whip and catch a few double thongs, not only to keep his hand in, but to be sure the thong is soft and mellow.

Many grooms hang their whips when they come in and leave them until just before they are needed for use, when they run over the thongs with a little pipe clay. This course makes a thong feel like pipe-clayed wire. Not only is it impossible to catch a thong properly when it is in this condition, but the tendency is to take the heart out of the leather, thus causing it to break at inopportune moments.

The very best treatment for a thong is to have it rubbed with a bullock's heart once a week or so. It can be dressed down in the meantime with mutton tallow or saddle soap.

The thong should always be so soft and pliable as to admit of doubling it sharply between the thumb and forefinger without apparent displacement of the

plaits. When in this condition it will cling to the
stick if well thrown, and can therefore be used, as
it is intended, for double thonging the wheelers.

It is well to watch the horses put to occasionally,
for very few grooms do this properly. In harnessing
a pair of horses unaided, a good coachman proceeds
about as follows :

Leading out his horses alternately, he puts the
harness on *quietly*, backing each horse when harnessed into a standing stall and fastening him by
both pillar reins, throwing a rug over his loins if the
temperature demands it. Then, after glancing over
his carriage to see that all is in readiness, he goes
to dress.

Let us glance for a moment at the horses as they
stand in their stalls with the harness on. We find
the general appearance good. The martingale, which
is often slouchily buckled on the outer edge of the
kidney link, is in this case either around the collar
or between the inner edge of the kidney link and
the collar. All the other parts look properly
fitted.

The traces are thrown over the horses' backs so
that the outside trace on both the near and the
off horse come on top. The outside or draught rein
is buckled into its bit, and we notice that the bits
hang easily and comfortably, the mouthpieces rest-

ing lightly on the plate of the mouth, not drawing the corners all out of shape and thereby torturing the poor beasts.

The inside or coupling rein is buckled into the noseband, buckle up, the point not being passed through the billet. The horse is led to his place by this coupling rein, to avoid touching the bit.

The fit of the collars is another most important point, and can not be too carefully attended to; they should not only be of proper length, but should also fit the horses' shoulders to a nicety. Each horse should have his own collar made for him. When the harness is put on, the collar should be stretched over the knee and put over the horse's head gently and comfortably to the animal. The hames, pad, etc., should be put on afterward. One often sees a groom forcing a tight collar over a horse's head with the hames buckled to it so that there is no yielding whatever. Is it to be wondered that those horses run back when the collars are held up before their faces?

The coachman has by this time returned, dressed, except as to his coat, hat, and gloves, and is wearing an apron to protect his immaculate white breeches. Leading his horses out by the noseband or coupling rein, he places them alongside the pole and buckles the coupling reins; he then passes the near horse's pole piece (strap) and buckles it in the point hole, which should be within six or eight inches of the point.

When the final poling-up is done the hole is, or should be, concealed by the carrier loops. (Nothing looks worse than to see the point of any strap sticking out some distance beyond the billet or loop which is intended as a guard for it; besides which, it is really dangerous in some cases. A projecting back strap on a four-in-hand lead harness is apt to catch the couplings, and trouble is quite likely to ensue.)

The off horse being thus loosely poled up, he fastens the traces, the outside one first, then the inside, repeating this with the near horse.

The outside trace is fastened first to avoid accident, for when the opposite is done a spirited horse is quite liable to whip around suddenly, and, with his inside trace fastened, may make things awkward.

For a somewhat similar reason the pole pieces are fastened loosely before the traces. Many consider this an unnecessary precaution, but let them think a moment.

Suppose that the last trace has just been fastened, and the pole pieces not even caught up. The off horse chancing to take a step forward brings the splinter bar in contact with his mate's haunches.

What is the natural result of such a performance, with horses that have any life?

The traces being properly fastened, the coachman proceeds to "pole them up," and in this work the judgment of the true coachman shows to advantage. The pole pieces should neither be too tight nor too loose, but it requires something of an artist to find the happy medium.

Some coachmen have an exceedingly faulty way of fastening their pole pieces; they twist the kidney link ring, and then, by passing the point of the strap upward through it, bring the buckle on top. This method makes an ugly distortion of the leather, besides weakening it by unnecessary side chafing.

The pole pieces should be put through the kidney link ring from the inside out (the ring hanging in its natural position). This brings the buckle into its proper place at the side, and the whole piece leads fair from the pole head, instead of showing what a sailor would describe as a "lubber's twist."

The horses being properly poled up, the coachman throws the hand piece of the near rein with the buckle end across the off horse's back, and, walking around to the off side, buckles the ends of the reins together. Then, doubling the hand pieces, he takes the bight, or portion of the reins at the doubling point, and passes it through the off pad terret and over the bearing-rein hook; the reins are then in a position to be easily taken for use, and are so placed that they are not liable to fall to the ground.

This done, he runs over his harness with a dry chamois, and brushes his horses' manes with the water brush. He then removes his apron, and, putting on his coat, hat, and gloves, bears up his horses and is ready to start out quietly.

Bearing reins are very necessary to almost all town driving, but they are to be used, not abused. They should be put on so as to keep the horse's head in its natural position, to prevent rubbing the bridle off or catching the cross bar of the bit when standing.

All lovers of horseflesh should be thankful that the heathenish custom of bearing a horse up outrageously high is very little practised now.

The method to be pursued in the harnessing of a four-in-hand is similar to that of a pair of horses, but there should always be at least two men to do it.

The chain which is used in place of the pole piece should be snapped into the kidney link (of course we presume one end of the chain to have been either snapped into or made fast to the pole head).

Experience teaches us that the wheelers' inside traces require to be a trifle shorter than the outside (about half a hole), to make the draught even. This is best accomplished by having the inside roller bolts covered with sufficient leather to take up the necessary amount of the traces. This makes extra holes in the traces unnecessary and avoids their consequent weakening.

The wheelers being properly put to, the leaders are brought up and coupled, their reins passed through the wheel turrets, the near one thrown to the off wheeler's pad. The traces are then fastened in the same manner as in pair-horse work, except that many lap or cross their inside traces instead of bringing them direct to their natural places. All this is a matter of personal fancy or experience.

The lead bars should never be fastened together with a chain or link, as is sometimes seen. This method might lead to the permanent injury of a horse were he to kick and get his leg between the main and side bars. A strap may, however, be used for this purpose with perfect propriety.

CHAPTER IX.

THERE are so many authorities who have treated the subject of driving thoroughly, that an extensive dissertation thereon is out of place. It may be well, however, to call attention to the fact that in driving, as in everything else, there is a right and a wrong way. It is much easier to commence properly than to correct bad habits.

It is therefore wise for a man who has had little or no experience to employ a competent instructor.

The seat on the box is the first thing to be learned ; after that, the manner of holding the reins and whip, and their proper manipulation.

The pupil must understand that the horse is not a machine, to which a certain amount of pressure is to be constantly applied in order to bring forth the necessary response.

The instructor will teach him to hold the hand quite close to the centre of the body, with the wrist slightly bent inward, the elbow nearly touching the side. In this position he will find it difficult, unless he is a powerful man, to apply a great amount of brute force to the reins. The hand and arm so placed form, as it were, a spring between the horse's mouth and the driver, thus precluding, to a great extent, the possibility of making a puller (either man or horse).

It is for this very reason that the American system of driving with a rein in each hand (except possibly in the case of trotting horses) is to be deprecated, because it inclines one to pull steadily against the bit, which sooner or later is sure to make the horse a puller.

As the pupil advances from single and pair horse work to the four-in-hand school, it may be well to call his attention to the fact that the mere "herding" of four horses over a road, even with a fair amount of form, is not driving, although it constantly passes for such.

The true coachman must study the individual characteristics of his horses, in order to bit and couple them to the best advantage. He must know how they are feeding, for in a team (of four horses) it is nothing unusual to have one horse which is slightly off, and therefore requires a certain amount of what a coachman calls "babying."

Nothing will give one more practice in work of this sort than the driving of a loaded coach thirty or forty miles a day, for several consecutive days, over our indifferent roads with the same team.*

Driving, by the Duke of Beaufort, covers the subject quite fully, and Howlett, in his Driving Lessons, gives an excellent and practical illustration of what we are about to describe. Swales, in his book, Driving, as I have Found It, gives some of the best sketches extant, showing the positions of the hands, with both two and four reins. Captain C. Morley Knight, in his Hints on Driving, also gives some very good suggestions. It would be well for any amateur coachman to read all these books at length, as they will undoubtedly prove of service to him.

Assuming the would-be coachman to be familiar with the method of holding his reins and proficient in the use of his whip, let him walk quietly up to his off wheeler. He finds the hand pieces of the reins either looped over the pad terret or with the bight pushed under the tug strap. The whip is either in the whip bucket or is laid across the wheelers' backs, both of

---

* In 1884 the author drove his coach, with the same team, 776 miles in exactly a month; starting from Long Island and driving up the Connecticut River Valley, over the White and Green Mountains, through the Berkshire Hills, and down the Hudson River to New York. The distance was taken from an odometer, of which a careful record was kept by one of the party. Hardly one month later the team competed in the National Horse Show and won a number of prizes. The coach loaded weighed something over five thousand pounds, there being eight in the party, besides three servants and the luggage.

which methods are well supported by competent authorities. Standing a little behind the off wheeler's pad, he faces a trifle toward the leaders and pulls the reins from their resting places, straightening them out carefully and separating lead from wheel. He then shortens the wheel reins gently until he all but feels his wheelers' mouths, proceeding in the same manner with the lead reins. He should avoid actually taking hold of his horses' mouths, for the giving them an " office," as it were, will make them restive. The reins being held in their proper position in the left hand, our friend takes up his whip (if on the wheelers' backs) with his right hand and transfers his reins from his left to his right.

He will note carefully the position of his leaders as to the lead bars, realizing that to this he must suit his length of rein in starting.

Being now ready to mount the box, he throws the ends of the reins over his right arm to keep them out of harm's way, gradually letting his off reins slip through his fingers to suit his change of position. (This method differs somewhat from that shown in Howlett's illustration, but will be found equally practical, as it allows the coachman to be in touch with his horses from the time he takes up his reins.)

He grasps the handle of the footboard with his right hand, then, putting his left foot on the hub of the wheel, his right on the roller bolt, and grasping the box rail with his left hand, he mounts the box. He remains standing only long enough to shift his reins from his right hand to his left. This done, he sits firmly on his cushion, letting the ends of his reins fall to the left of his knees. Assuring himself that he has a proper pressure on each rein, he warns his load that he is about to start, and, with a nod to the men at the horses' heads, he gently feels his leaders' mouths to put them on the alert. This will bring them to their bits with their traces hanging easily. The wheelers are then given their office, and, if the team is a handy one, they will go up to their collars, and with a word of encouragement, together with the slightest dropping of the hand, the whole team will start the coach without any plunging or jibbing.

It is very unworkmanlike (unless absolutely necessary) to let the leaders start the coach with the wheelers not in their collars; and it is nearly as bad to see the wheelers shoving the bars on the leaders' haunches. Many a young coachman feels that he wants to start out with a flourish and all on the jump. He will learn, however, that the good coachman gets under way as quietly as possible, in order to accustom his horses to working in unison. It is all well enough on the smooth, level road, but let the start be up a steep hill with a heavy load, and we will see our young friend's horses rearing and jibbing, but making no progress, while the quietly driven team starts off together without apparent effort. Our young friend will probably say, "Oh, my horses are so high-strung!" But if he thinks over the matter he will probably recollect that he dropped his hand suddenly, giving each horse full rein, at the same time flourishing his whip or giving a loud cluck. His horses with different degrees of promptness sprang to their work, and, finding a solid weight too great for any one of them to start alone, began the seesaw act. When once a team is in this condition, the only thing to do is to quiet them down; let them stand a few moments, and then see if they can't be started by more temperate management.

Many a young coachman will miscalculate the distance in which the pulling up of a team can be comfortably accomplished, and will be quite surprised to find that it takes some little experience to acquire judgment in so doing.

The horses coming up at a round trot should be slowed gradually, but not taken back to a walk a few feet short of the spot, nor brought up so fast that they will either require to be thrown on their haunches or allowed to go some distance beyond their objective point before they are brought to a stop.

Howlett gives a most excellent illustration of the method of making what he calls a "dead stop."

Nimrod, in his chapter on Gentlemen Coachmen,

in Annals of the Road, gives another method, which, while not quite as finished in appearance, is most practical and workmanlike; we will quote it for the convenience of our readers. " When all four horses are to be restrained at once, almost all coachmen draw all the reins through their fingers at the same moment. This is not the way to do it, for here your horses' mouths are lost. The coachman should change his hands thus : He should open the fingers of his right hand and put the reins into them, about two inches in front of his left hand, and then catch them again with his left by passing it beyond his right. By this plan his horses' mouths, as I have said before, are not lost, which they would otherwise be. I am indebted to Jack Peer for this wrinkle, which I briefly noted in my last."

The team being finally pulled up, the coachman shifts his reins from his left to his right hand, taking them short enough to allow of their reaching comfortably to the handle of the footboard, not so slack that they will fret the wheelers, and throws the ends of his reins over his right arm. He now puts his left foot backward to the step on the boot, grasping meanwhile the box rail with his left hand, then lowers himself until his right foot is placed on the roller bolt, at the same time grasping the handle on the footboard with his right hand; then placing his left foot on the hub of the wheel, he descends to mother earth holding the reins and whip high enough to prevent their annoying the wheelers. He now assumes the position first described in taking up the reins, and shifts his reins from his right to his left hand, lays his whip over the wheelers' backs, and draws the bight of the reins through the loop of the tug, when his labours are at an end.

It is necessary for a true coachman to know the component parts of his harness thoroughly, be it single or pair-horse, tandem or four-horse.

The best way to become familiar with the different parts is to have the harness placed in a heap, every strap unbuckled, then to put it together unassisted. This will probably take some considerable time, but observation will show reasons for the existence of certain parts which seem useless.

If any part of the harness seems unduly chafed as compared with the rest, it is probably due to bad fitting. The ability to remedy such a defect will afford some satisfaction.

CHAPTER X.

THERE is very little to be said on this subject, as the accompanying photographs show the desired points far more clearly than mere verbal description.

The coachman's livery, shown in Plates XXXV and XXXVI, will be seen to differ from that of the groom, shown in Plates XXXVII and XXXVIII, in a few details. For example, the coachman's body coat should have six buttons in front and flaps on the pockets, two buttons at the waist behind and two very near the bottom of the skirt. The groom's body coat should have five or six buttons in front, no flaps to the pockets, and six buttons behind, generally placed as in Plate XXXVIII. Two very excellent examples of the above liveries are shown, as they vary a little in some trifling ways. It will be noticed, however, that in both examples the coachman's coat is quite a bit longer in the skirt than that of the groom. All of the boots shown here are good examples, and have not the tendency to fall down and disappear like the bellows of an ac-

Plate XXXV: Coachman in Livery (Front and Rear View).

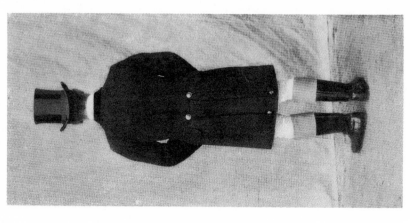

Plate XXXVI: Coachman in Livery
(Front and Rear View)

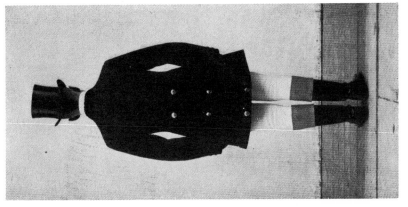

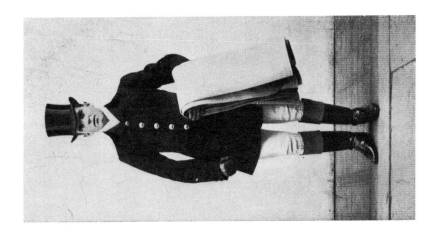

Plate XXXVII: Groom in Livery (Front and Rear View).

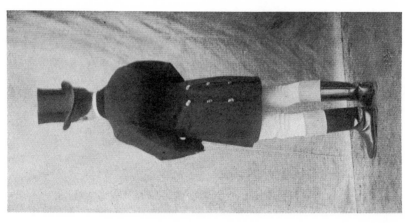

Plate XXXVIII : Groom in Livery

cordion, which is often noticed. The breeches are all well-made leathers, and on the average well put on. The upper buttons at the knees should invariably be placed in a hollow which is found on the outside of the tibia and just below the patella or kneecap. These liveries all happen to have velvet collars; they are simply a matter of individual taste. Cockades should be worn only when the owner is a member of the army, navy, or diplomatic corps. Shoulder knots and fancy collars and cuffs are not in the best of form. It may be well here to state that a footman in house livery is quite proper on a lady's carriage, especially when the carriage is an open one.

Plate XXXIX shows a coachman and groom in greatcoats, and the same features will be found here as in the body coats, except that, as the coat buttons to the neck, the coachman's coat has generally two rows of seven buttons and that of the groom two rows of six buttons, but they may have the same number.

As a general rule a coachman's greatcoat should come a trifle below the top of his boots, and that of the groom to the upper button of his breeches when placed as before described. Plate V, in the chapter on Coaching, gives a very good example of a guard's livery.

Plate XL shows two styles of stable clothes or undress liveries. It should be remembered that where a roundabout coat is used the low hat is appropriate, and the high one with the tail coat.

We give here a list of the articles with which each servant should be equipped:

One silk hat; one felt storm hat, or second hat dressed for purpose; one Derby; one suit of stable clothes, made either of whipcord or tweed; one sleeved waistcoat; one heavy cover coat; one stable cap; one mackintosh (or an upper Benjamin); one dozen collars; one dozen neckcloths; one livery body coat; one stripped valencia waistcoat (with sleeves); one livery great coat; one pair of trousers to match same (for *occasional* use in the morning or at night); one pair leathers (or cloth breeches); one pair top boots, with trees for same; one pair dogskin gloves; one pair heavy wool-lined gloves; one pair woolen gloves; one pair breeches trees.

HORSE CLOTHING.

Plate XLI shows a horse in undress or night clothing. This happens to be a very good sporting pattern, being of fawn with alternate stripes of red and black. Blankets of plain fawn, or with a red and black check on a fawn ground, are almost

Plate XXXIX : Coachman and Groom in Greatcoats.

Plate XL: Undress Liveries.

Plate XLI : Horse in Night Clothing.

Plate XLII: Horse in Dress Clothing.

equally smart. If initials are used with any of these patterns they should be placed over the hips. It will be noticed here that the groom is wearing such a costume as is appropriate to the purpose, while in Plate XLII, which follows, he is more trimmed into shape conformably to the dress clothing worn by his horse. While undress clothing is ordinarily made with the rug all in one piece, the dress clothing has what is called a quarter or loin cloth, which goes to the shoulders; a breastplate, which is strapped to it at the crown of the withers and covers the horse's chest; and a small pad cloth, which goes under the roller. There is also a small breast girth, which buckles to the roller to keep the whole from slipping back. In addition to a roller there should be a surcingle without padding, which can be used when the clothing is thrown over a saddle.

QUARTER CLOTHS.

These are of two varieties : dress and sporting. The former are made of cloth or leather, and shaped for throwing over the loins or for use under the harness for protection in cold weather. (If monograms or crests are used they should be small and unostentatious.) The latter are simply a square of a woollen material, generally striped fawn, which are folded in two and thrown over the loins when the horses are standing.

APRONS AND CARRIAGE RUGS.

Aprons are commonly made of a light-drab box cloth or Bedford cord. Those for an owner's use are faced with leather, generally pigskin, at the bottom, inside; are lined with some plaid worsted material, and have in front at the top a flap which covers a couple of pockets. In the centre of the top is placed a medallion for a monogram or crest. This has a strap made fast to it on the under side with which to fasten it to the seat rail. Such an apron as the above described is intended for two persons.

The four-horse or tandem coachman's apron is made of any suitable material to strap around the waist and to come about to the ankle when standing. It has no medallion or flap.

A pair of smart aprons for use in a dogcart are made of dressed deerskin and box cloth, with the flap and medallion as above described.

Lap robes for use in a light wagon are made of cloth, which either matches the lining of the wagon or is of light drab.

Aprons for servants' use are made of heavy box cloth lined in the same colour. They should be about the shade of the box cushion, which is always of some dark colour. When drab greatcoats are used, an apron of the same colour is often seen. This should never be. As far as the rugs for use inside the carriages are concerned, individual fancy may dictate, provided it does not run to knitted worsted or to some gay colour.

Aprons and rugs should ordinarily be folded outside out, as in this way the inside is more certain of being clean when thrown over the knees.

CHAPTER XI.

THE STABLE.

THERE are a great many minor details, mere trifles in themselves, and of no moment as far as labour and expense are concerned, which go far toward giving the stable that finish and smartness so much sought after by those who take an interest in such matters.

Even a most commonplace interior, by a judicious use of a few yards of an inexpensive material and some nails, can be made to appear well cared for; and a few days' work by a carpenter will make the roughest barn look quite workmanlike inside.

The steels, whips, horse boots, etc., by a little taste in arrangement may be made really decorative; and the horse clothing, carriage rugs, and aprons all do their part when properly disposed.

Straw mats, which can be rolled up at night, either made by the servant or purchased at the feed store, together with some white sea sand, give character to any stable. An occasional stencil of coloured paints showing either the monogram or crest of the owner, looks quite well on a neatly sanded floor.

All these little niceties help to give a servant some pride in his work, and, if he is keen, one will see every now and then some trifling improvement which he has found time to make in his spare moments. Even the owner who takes no interest in his stable will feel a certain amount of satisfaction in realizing that it is kept up "shipshape and Bristol fashion."

When there is sufficient time, all the steel-tined forks should be kept clean and burnished, the shovels, rakes, etc., varnished or whitened, and the judicious use of a little paint on these articles sometimes adds to their appearance.

Everything for stable use should have its place and be kept there. This place must not be merely a dark shelf in some dusty, musty closet, but a rack, hook, or shelf suited to each article, in plain sight, and so placed as to improve rather than detract from the general appearance. The larger stable tools (forks, brooms, etc.) present a most slovenly appearance when either piled carelessly in a corner or distributed " all over the place," so to speak. These can be made to furnish considerably by hanging them close together on some bit of exposed wall, making a panel of them, as it were. So it is with practically every article intended for use in the stable at large.

The outside of all the boxes and bottles used in cleaning, etc., should be kept tidy, being wiped off and covered directly after using. The piece of cloth, sponge, or brush belonging to each should be neatly placed by its side. A servant who has not been properly trained to this sort of thing will often say that he " hasn't time for such nonsense." If after he has tried it he is still dissatisfied, get another. Of course there is a limit to the powers of each of us " poor human beings," and the foregoing advice might in some cases be an injustice to a really hard-working man, but on the average it will be found to be sound.

The necessity for every horse owner to inform himself as to the time the various branches of stable work should consume can not be sufficiently emphasized ; such knowledge will enable him to criticise his servants justly, thereby avoiding much of the friction which is engendered either through thoughtlessness or lack of knowledge on the part of the employer who administers an undeserved reproof.

The question often arises as to the number of men stables of various sizes should employ. Such a question is not easily answered, for the conditions differ widely. As a general rule, one man besides the coachman to every four horses is a good proportion, and with proper management should suffice in the average establishment.

In a large stable a great deal of the comfort and economy of running is dependent on the head coachman and his ability to train his undermen to their respective duties, besides keeping them up to the mark in other ways.

One of the very important points in the keeping of a healthy lot of horses lies in an early morning feed, thereby giving the animals time to properly digest their meal before they are called upon to go to work. A competent coachman will at least superintend the feeding, and will always attend to the doling out of each horse's rations himself; there is no other possible way of his accomplishing the desired result.

In another chapter, the coachman who simply fed his nags their mess of oats regularly and gave them bran mash on Saturdays is referred to as a duffer, and yet it is painful to realize that many such duffers exist. An intelligent man knows that a horse can not be kept in the bloom of condition by any such treatment, especially one with a delicate appetite. The food must be varied, and made easily digestible by crushing the grain and chopping the hay. In winter an occasional feed of steamed food or warm gruel is most nutritious, as are also carrots, beets, turnips, etc. Corn, wheat, rye, and barley crushed can at times be used, mixed with the oats, with good results, and in many little ways, such as salting, moistening, etc., a mess can be made more palatable. Hay should be fed sparingly to horses which are hard worked, but the old theory that oats, and oats alone, are the only food for hard-worked ones is an exploded one, for there is no surer though slow means of, so to speak, "burning up" a horse.

When possible, a few bites of green grass will be of benefit, as it will assist in keeping the digestive organs in good condition. Watering should not be carelessly done. While some persons go to excess in depriving their horses of water, it is certainly wise to limit them somewhat, excepting possibly at evening. A horse should never drink his fill before going to work on the road, and the variety of the work will be, in a way, a guide as to the quantity to be allowed. It is scarcely necessary to add that when a horse is heated and about to be stabled, no more than a sponging should be given until he is thoroughly cooled out.

This chapter is not intended in any way as a treatise on feeding, but merely to show that it is a subject admitting of, and in fact requiring, considerable judgment and experience.

In addition to careful feeding, it is necessary that a horse's teeth should be watched and kept in good order. Many a case of debilitated condition, pulling, side reining, rearing, etc., is due to a bad state of the mouth, which, when neglected, causes permanent trouble.

Passing from the care of horses to that of the har-

ness and carriages, it may be well to call attention to
the great difference in the care bestowed upon them by
coachmen generally and individually. It is exceedingly
interesting to go to some of our coachbuilders and carefully examine carriages which are up for some slight
repair. The exception is the one which has had careful attention while in use.

There is a tendency toward the neglect of a
proper care of the axles and boxes, either in allowing
sand or some rough substance to scratch the surface,
or in neglecting to wipe the oil from the woodwork,
which results in a rapid rotting. In England it is customary to have the axles attended to altogether by
the coachbuilder, and such a practice is strongly to
be advised, as it will cost but a few dollars a year, and
one is thereby assured as to their condition.

Some coachmen take pains always to have on hand
a pot of black varnish and a little paint the colour of
their carriages, so as to touch up the steps or any
trifling scratches which detract from the general appearance. Others bring in carriages which have not
had nearly as much use, and which look shabby from
mere lack of proper care; in fact, they often show
signs of having been actually neglected. A carriage
should never be left overnight without a careful washing. Plenty of water should be used, but by no means
is this to be applied with a hose. Two large sponges

should be provided, one to be used on the panels, etc., and the other on the undercarriage. When the mud shows a tendency to harden, a sponge full of water should be gently sopped against it until it is so softened that it may be wiped off without scratching the surface. Hot water must not be used on any account, as it is ruinous to the varnish. A wet chamois should be used after the carriage has been carefully sponged, providing, of course, every bit of sand and grit has already been removed. A damp or wet cloth or sponge should never be used on the morocco upholstering of a carriage.

The practice of using soap around the axles and hub is prevalent with many coachmen, and can not be too severely condemned; a little turpentine may be used to remove the grease. Many of them also have the habit of swashing the water *all over* the carriage, regardless of the trimming and the various interstices, which results in the bulging of many a panel. There is what is termed a well-hole in the door of any heavy carriage with window glass, which furnishes a ready receptacle for water. Most coachbuilders put a couple of small holes at the bottom of the door to furnish an outlet for the water; but coachmen rarely keep these holes clear, generally allowing them to fill up with dirt and sand, thus rendering them useless for the purpose for which they are intended.

It is well to caution the coachman to wrap his wrench and the other implements which he may carry in the carriage in a cloth, as they are often the cause of some apparently inexplicable rattling.

It is cheapest, in the long run, to have carriages which are in constant use sent to the coachbuilder for varnishing, examination, etc., at least once a year; and carriages which have been allowed to stand unused in the stable for several months should always be examined by a coachbuilder, and any trifles which require attention should be adjusted before they run again. The loosening of a single nut, and any trifling accumulation of rust between the leaves of the springs, will cause a squeaking and rattling, and are often productive of more serious trouble.

It is therefore "penny wise and pound foolish" to neglect these things. Nothing affects a carriage more injuriously than a damp coach house, as the swelling of the wood is liable to burst the panels, etc. Where a coachman is aware that his coach house is somewhat damp, he should be particular to stand his carriages away as far as possible from any stone or brick wall, so that they may have the freest possible circulation of air.

Unless this subject has been given close attention, it is difficult to have the slightest conception of the many little ways in which a poor coachman can run up an endless coachmaker's bill, causing much annoyance; whereas, if his part of the work had been properly understood and attended to, this would have been in a great measure obviated.

It is much the same in the care of harness. One man will keep a harness in good condition for five or six years, while another will ruin it in six months. Never allow the use of any harness polish or varnish, unless on a very old harness, for there is no better way of taking the heart out of the leather. A blacking or composition should be used which has considerable oil in it, and is applied moist and polished with the combination of elbow-grease and a brush. The application of beeswax is also beneficial. The same criticisms as to care, etc., may be made with regard to the saddles, bridles, steels, breeches, boots, etc. It should be remembered that while one coachman who really understands these duties and attends to them properly is well worth good wages, for he is an economy to his employer, another, through his ignorance, may be an extravagance at half the money.

The photographs of stable interiors which are given here show good examples of neatly kept establishments. Plate XLIV shows a harness room in a stable in which only one man is kept; but that man is an excellent one, who has been for many years in his place, and has had

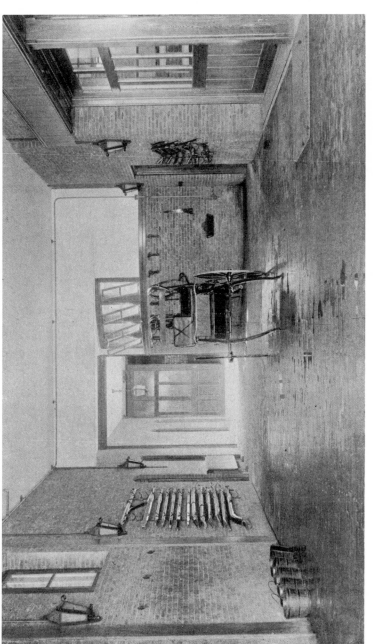

Plate XLIII : Washstand in a Large Stable.

Plate XLIV : Harness Room in

Plate XLV: Harness Room in Town Stable.

Plate XLVI: Harness Room in Large Stable

Plate XLVII : Coach-Room Interior.

Plate XLVIII : Coach-Room Interior.

the advantage of serving an employer who takes unusual interest in appointments.

No attempt has been made to describe the various minutiæ shown in these photographs, for, after a certain point is reached, so much in the arrangement and general treatment depends on the owner's personal taste that we have used the illustrations more with the view of showing some good examples than of defining any one particular method.

Convenience and the sanitary conditions are the two points mainly to be considered in the building of a stable. Ventilation must be carefully looked after, and should be so arranged that when desired there can be a free circulation of air in the stable without exposing its occupants to a direct draught.

The coach house should invariably be separated from the stable by closed doors, and, if possible, by a separately ventilated antechamber or harnessing room. The ammonia from the stables is very injurious to carriages, and, in addition to this, its odour permeates the carriages and is very disagreeable.

The use of tiling in interior stable work is much to be recommended, as it can be thoroughly washed, thereby reducing the possibility of contagion among the horses to the lowest point.

The question as to what flooring is best for the stalls always brings forth a variety of opinions. Where sta-

bles in the country are so situated as to allow the use
of good clay bottoms in the loose boxes, there is no
better or more healthy flooring for a horse to
stand upon, provided, of course, they are properly
attended to and frequently renovated. In the average town stable, where the horses are kept in standing
stalls, a slat flooring made of some soft wood, such as
white pine, and draining slightly to a grated trough at
the rear of the stalls, is most practical. It is wisest to
have this floor laid with solid planks on either side next
the partitions, and three or four loose planks or slats
about three inches wide laid half an inch apart to fill
up the centre. The solid planks should be put down in
concrete or asphalt, to allow of no crevices.

The question as to the width of the stalls depends
somewhat upon the size of the horses kept. The average idea seems to be that four feet six inches is the
width for any and every stall. The author's personal
experience, after quite extensive experiments, inclines
him to believe that this width is just about proper to
insure an average-sized horse becoming cast when he
attempts to roll, and that it is better to have the stall
either so narrow (about four feet wide) as to prevent
the animal from trying to roll, or so wide (about five
feet) as to reduce the chances of casting to a minimum.

The suggestion as to the use of soft woods for
the stall floors will be found a sound one, for they

Plate XLIX : Coach-Room Interior.

Plate L: Stable Interior.

Plate LI: Stable Interior.

Plate LII : Stable Interior.

Plate LIII : Stable Interior.

Plate LIV : Stable Interior.

Plate LIVa: Stable Interior.

Plate LV : Burnishing Pole Chains.

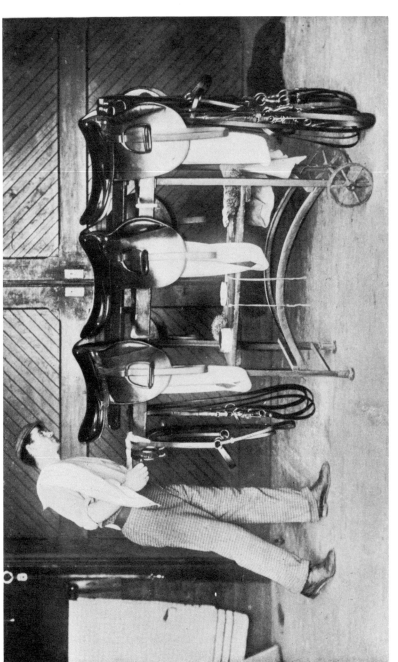

Plate LVI: Movable Saddle Back.

are elastic to a certain degree, and much less injurious to horses' feet than either hard wood, concrete, or asphalt. Of course they wear out much sooner, but can be easily replaced.

The size of the harness room and its arrangement depend, of course, entirely upon that of the rest of the stable. It should be kept dry at all times, and for this reason must be provided with a stove or other means of heating which can be used on damp days even in summer.

CHAPTER XII.

IT occasionally happens that a novice wishes to start some sort of a stable, but his ignorance of the subject makes the undertaking both difficult and unnecessarily costly. In the generality of cases such a person buys at random and is almost sure to repent at leisure.

It is to be hoped that the suggestions included in this chapter may be found of some benefit.

We will consider the question first from the standpoint of a man who wishes to "turn out" a single brougham, although the suggestions given here are equally adapted to any standard vehicle.

The question of dollars and cents comes first, and after that it is wise to consider whether the first purchase shall be individual, or is intended as the nucleus of a large stable. What is worth doing at all is worth doing well, and for this reason one should not attempt the turning out of the simplest kind of equipage unless he intends to do it properly.

It is well for those who are not inclined to give the matter close attention, or, in other words, to take the necessary trouble connected therewith, to patronize the livery stable.

The selection of a carriage which "fills the bill" should be the first consideration, and to that can be added a suitable horse, harness, etc. Of course there are many enthusiasts who buy a "clinker" whenever and wherever they run across him, without regard to size, type, etc. Such persons must necessarily buy their carriages to suit their horses. It is almost superfluous to call attention to the fact that the pursuance of this method requires both large means and an elaborately run stable.

And, by the way, these are not the only requirements, for such purchasers should have the knowledge and experience to enable them to carry out the establishment, else they are almost certain to make serious blunders. It is therefore a good plan for any one who has had little or no experience, whether his means are ample or only moderate, to begin very slowly and work up to, rather than launch out in, a large establishment.

Let us suppose that a gentleman, whose means are somewhat limited, is about to "set up" a single brougham. He has a nice little stable, and wishes to do everything properly and as economically as possible. Being without experience, he is somewhat at sea.

To begin with, let him interest a friend who really knows, and who will help him in the looking up of a second-hand carriage of good make and shape. After considerable search such an one is found, shabby in appearance, it is true, but which can be bought at a low figure. The purchase does not seem particularly attractive to our friend, but being so advised, he decides to make it. The carriage is then sent to a good shop, where it is stripped of its paint, and, if necessary, of its trimmings. In the course of six or eight weeks it is repainted and re-lined, and having undergone a careful examination, is to all intents and purposes quite as good as a new carriage, provided, of course, it was originally of first-class construction. The entire cost to our friend is probably between six hundred and eight hundred dollars—not much more than half the price of a first-class new carriage. All persons with ex-perience in such matters will agree that they would rather have an old carriage by a good maker than a new one of cheaper construction.

Directly the purchase of the carriage is made he requests his well-posted friend to look him up a good horse about seven years old, between fifteen two and sixteen hands high, and weighing from eleven hundred to twelve hundred pounds, suitable for his brougham. In the absence of his friend he applies to some dealer of good repute, and outlining his wants, places himself in the dealer's hands. Confidence of this sort is very seldom misplaced, for there is honour even among the constantly maligned horse dealers.

The man who, knowing very little about horses, poses as an expert, is almost invariably "played for all he is worth." Very, very few amateurs are competent to cope with experienced horse dealers, but many undertake the task, and the dealers very naturally consider these persons "fair game," and treat them on the "dog-eat-dog" principle. Who can wonder that the result is generally more favourable to the seller than to the buyer?

Many an amateur who is most willing to advise a friend in the purchase of horseflesh would, were he going down into his own pocket, call in his coachman, veterinarian, and all available talent, and even then would buy with considerable hesitation.

Our friend ultimately secures a good horse for something like three hundred dollars, and either leaves him with the dealer or sends him to a livery stable until his own stable is in readiness. He then buys a first-class harness from a reliable maker or importer for about one hundred and fifty dollars, for the purchase of a second-hand or inferior harness is the poorest of economies.

The finding of a capable servant will probably take time; none should be engaged without a personal reference. Chapter X gives a list of the articles necessary for the servant, and at the end of this chapter will be found a list of the articles necessary in the stable where one or more horses are kept. The latter list will undoubtedly appal an inexperienced person, but there is really nothing included in the entire summary which can be conveniently dispensed with. Of course there are a number of articles which would not require duplication were there several horses instead of one. If the gentleman in question is a practical man and really interested in his new departure, he will have all these things provided before his servant arrives, and will as far as possible find out the use of each article.

The horse, brougham, and harness are now sent home and the servant instructed to report for duty. The first day or so will have to be spent in "getting things to rights." On the second afternoon our friend takes a short drive, realizing that his horse is not "fit," and should be used very moderately for some time. Later, when everything is running smoothly, he takes occasion to drive directly to the stable on a muddy day, and superintends the doing up of the horse, carriage, etc.   He is probably surprised at the amount of time consumed, and, realizing that the carriage did not reach home till about half past one in the morning, it occurs to him to wonder what time John got to bed.   The appreciation of such matters is very necessary to an owner who is desirous of doing justice to a conscientious servant, as well as of keeping a lax one up to the mark.

Oftentimes a man of means who takes no interest in horseflesh desires to establish a stable which will be suited to his family needs.   He wishes to keep enough horses to warrant a free use of his carriages, and yet the mere details are sufficiently formidable to deter him from the undertaking.

It may not be amiss to give here the "condiments," so to speak, of a good-sized private stable which contains vehicles of the useful sort, and the servants, horses, etc., necessary to its maintenance.

We will suppose this establishment to be intended for city use in winter, and for such a place as Newport in the summer.   The most important factor is the coachman, who should be a near approach in qualifications to the man who is described in Chapter VII as a head coachman.   Such a man is not always to be had for the asking, but it will be found wise to wait until he can be secured.

The question as to the necessary carriages, horses,

harness, etc., hinges largely upon the size of the
family and the amount of entertaining done. The
brougham and victoria naturally are the first selected, then the landau, and after that an omnibus
and *vis-a-vis* or similar carriage. To these may be
added a runabout, some sort of two-wheeler, and
perhaps a phaëton. To horse such an establishment
properly at least six horses will be necessary; they
should be so nearly of a size as to be interchange-
able; the wisest policy being to have three in the
neighbourhood of fifteen three hands high, with
some quality and action for use in the brougham,
victoria, phaëton, etc., and three about sixteen hands
high, for use in the omnibus, single brougham, and
landau. Such a lot should make up quite a decent
four on a pinch. It is sometimes wise to keep a
couple of ordinary nags for night work, but this
is not an absolute necessity.

It is presumed, of course, that the carriages are
to be called upon morning, noon, and night, and in
consequence the stable force must be sufficiently large.
Whether it shall be two or three in number depends
somewhat upon whether a stable servant is required
besides the coachman at all times.

The coachman should not be above taking a hand
when necessary; but it is unreasonable to suppose
that a man who is often on the box from 9 A. M.

Plate LVII.: Articles necessary for the Washstand.

Plate LVIII: Some Stable Necessaries.

till 1 P. M., from 2 P. M. till 6 P. M., and from eight in the evening till one or two in the morning, can do much work himself when such is the case, and provision must be made accordingly. Many a good man has been driven to the use of stimulants purely from the lack of consideration by his employer.

NECESSARIES FOR ONE HORSE.

The following lists embody the articles necessary in the stable, for the horse, for the carriage, for the harness, and for the livery, and are named under their respective headings for the convenience of the reader:

FOR THE STABLE.

One stable broom; one ordinary broom; one long-handled feather duster; two oak pails; one shovel; one steel-tined hayfork (for hayloft); one wooden hayfork (for stable); one manure fork; one manure basket; one squeegee; one barrel of white sand.

FOR THE HORSE.

One body brush; one dandy brush; one water brush; one horse foot tub; one currycomb; one mane comb; one pair large trimming shears; one pair of clipping shears; one hoof brush; one hoof pick; one can of neat's-foot oil; one pair of felt soaking boots; right and left ankle boots (felt); one four-quart measure; one sieve (one sixteenth inch mesh); one scraper; two thick night blankets; one thick day blanket (preferably a full suit); one thin night blanket; one thin day blanket; one night surcingle; one day surcingle; one leather head collar; one web stall collar (white); six stable rubbers; one set woollen bandages; one set stockinet bandages.

FOR THE CARRIAGE.

One short-handled feather duster (fine); one hair broom; one wheel jack; two sponges; one chamois (to wet); one chamois (to use dry); six stable dusters; one box brass polish; one box axle grease or oil; one box carriage candles.

FOR THE HARNESS.

Two holly or buckthorn whips; two crest brushes; one set blacking brushes; one harness sponge; one chamois (dry); one black chamois; one chain burnisher, also burnishing bag; one bottle black paint and brush; one box harness blacking; one can of sweet oil; one box of saddle paste; one box saddle soap; one jar of Crown soap; two bars of castile soap; one bottle of Meltonian cream (for patent leather); one set of oval punches; two or three Crew punches; one hook for hanging harness when cleaning.

FOR THE LIVERY.

One hat brush; one set blacking brushes; one pair boot-top brushes; one breeches ball; one box breeches paste; one pair rubber boots for servant; one rubber washing apron; one box or bottle shoe blacking or oil; one bottle boot-top fluid; one bottle boot-top polish or one box boot-top paste and one box boot-top powder; one button stencil plate (for cleaning livery buttons).

CHAPTER XIII.

BITS AND BITTING.

A LENGTHY and exhaustive treatment of this subject would of itself require a special work, so that we will only glance at the question as applied to the average "green" horse which is purchased for harness purposes to-day.

He is generally trained "to go" in harness, and that is about all that can be said, for the bitting and mouthing are almost absolutely neglected.

Ordinarily speaking, the farmer who raises him puts him into his wagons or plow for a season's work, and is perfectly well satisfied if the animal goes in the direction designated, no matter how. The horse is then sold to a city buyer and landed in such a place as our New York "Bull's Head." Here the first consideration is a quick sale, and some heavy-handed, beefy individual is put behind him and pulls as hard as he can on the reins to "make him show," forcing him meanwhile up to the bit by the vigorous use of a whalebone whip. The result of all this is that when the horse is finally purchased he has practically no mouth whatever. It is much more difficult to bit such an animal so that he will go pleasantly than it is to accomplish the same result with an altogether unbroken one.

Fortunately, the growing demand for the fancy type of carriage horse has led some of the more practical dealers to take manners into consideration, which means that they must keep a horse some few weeks before they attempt to sell him. Such men are a benefit to the driving public ; and the additional increase in their prices over those of the dealer who sells in the rough state is to a great extent warranted. They generally have to carry their horses through the distemper, which attacks almost all unacclimated ones, thereby increasing both their feed bills and their percentage of mortality.

On taking a horse from " Bull's Head," for example, it will be well to do nothing but nurse him, " lounge " him, and bit him for at least the first month. He is generally dosed with arsenic or some artificial flesh-producing food, and if put to work at once will rarely thrive. After he has been rested for a day or two and thoroughly purged, the bitting harness, which is shown in Plate LIX, should be used for a few days. This is practically what is employed in the first breaking in of a colt. If it is left on the horse for an hour or so daily when in a loose box, it will accustom him to the finding of a comfortable position for his head when held in restraint, and will tend to develop the necessary muscles.

The bit should be a snaffle, with iron keys or tassels attached, and should be dropped comparatively low in the mouth, for in this position it has a tendency to encourage flexion and yielding.

After a couple of weeks of treatment with the bitting harness, during which time the pupil may be given leading exercise, it is well to begin the use of the dumb jockey and cavesson (Plate LX). The modern dumb jockey is made with two hard-rubber arms, each extending upward and outward from the centre of the pad ; these are furnished with eyes into which the side reins, etc., can be fastened. These side reins are made partly of rubber, so that they will yield to a comparatively light pressure, thereby to a great extent obviating the danger of a "dead pull." The horse very soon finds that his head and mouth are more comfortable and easy when he yields to the pressure exerted by the elasticity of the rubber, and consequently drops his head into the position which gives him that relief. This is exactly similar to the result which a man with excellent hands is able to accomplish, and which is so much to be desired.

The cavesson is no more nor less than a rigid noseband to which rings are attached on the front and

Plate LIX : Horse with Bitting Harness.

Plate LX: Horse with Dumb Jockey
and Cavesson.

sides, and into which the "lounging" reins, side reins, or other straps can be buckled at the pleasure of the breaker, in order to accustom the horse to restraint aside from that of the bit. This is a most useful instrument in the hands of a skilful person, but it can be made very injurious when improperly applied.

Having given the horse several days of the dumb jockey, he may be led or lounged with the cavesson. It will be noticed that the treatment has already brought him into better balance. An intelligent use of soft ground and thick straw, with occasional logs among it which can be seen, will add very materially to his action and carriage.

The above-described treatment will be found of considerable service when the horse is finally put in harness, provided his driver conforms to the principles which govern it. The animal must be made to realize that by flexing his neck to a certain point he will find relief, but that the harder he pulls the more he will suffer. The application of this principle is of equal service in the bitting of a horse and in the making of a coachman's hands.

One of the most brilliant exponents of the school of flexing and mouthing was the Frenchman Baucher; and while his attention was in a great measure directed toward the training of the horse for the saddle and manege, he nevertheless applied methods in the accomplishment of his work which are of inestimable value to a horseman. One of his first principles was to teach the horse to play with the bit, thus keeping his mouth moist and distracting his attention from a possible inclination to "take hold."

The perfectly mannered harness horse should simply carry the bit in his mouth; it should be felt by the coachman at all times, but with a touch so light that it would not break a piece of thin twine.

The proper adjustment of the noseband is much neglected, and in most harnesses this important strap has but one or two buckle holes. One should depend almost as much on the noseband as on the bit to make a pulling horse go pleasantly. It is far wiser to tighten the noseband when one's horse is pulling than to take up the curb chain. The tighter the curb chain is fastened the more senseless the mouth becomes, until finally one can make almost no impression on the poor brute. Should a horse be pulling, it is well to try the effect of dropping the bit one or two holes and having the curb chain easy (not too loose), to tighten the noseband so that the mouth is kept closed.

Avoid severe bitting as far as possible, for there is nothing pleasanter than a pliant snaffle bridle mouth; but whatever bit is used, avoid placing it always in the same position, thereby making the mouth "dead." Often and often a horse which will pull your arms out on the lower bar of the curb will go gently and lightly on a leather or rubber covered snaffle. Pulling in a young horse is frequently caused by some tooth discomfort, which can easily be remedied, when a pleasant mouth is the result.

Many of our readers will doubtless claim an inconsistency between the advice given above and that contained in the chapter on Harness and Harnessing, which advocates the use of Buxton bits, pulley bridoons, etc., at certain times. These apparently severe bits, when properly used on a horse which understands them, are in reality not severe at all; but when put for the first time on a horse which has not been educated by dumb jockey training, etc., they may indeed be made instruments of torture.

Let all remember that no horse is fit to run in a lady's carriage, or, in fact, in any park equipage, until he possesses good manners, and that such good manners are only brought about by a thorough education on the lines above described.

CHAPTER XIV.

This much-mooted subject seems deserving of a chapter by itself, and while the author feels that bearing reins can very properly be used and not abused, that there are times when they are essential and times when they are more than superfluous, he prefers to put his personal views to one side and to allow the reader to form his own opinion, either from experience or from the criticisms of the well-known coachmen who are quoted below. The quotations cover a period of fifty years, and show that during that time there has been considerable diversity of opinion on the question at issue.

The Duke of Beaufort, in Driving, says: "From long experience, and having saved many broken knees by their use, we advocate bearing reins—especially in single harness—put on with sense and discretion, so as never to be so short as to annoy a horse in any way, and always when standing for any time to be unborne."

Major Dixon and others, in the chapter on The

Coach House, Harness Room, and Driving Appliances, in the Badminton Driving, say : "Bearing reins have been, and will always continue to be, a bone of contention between coachmen of different classes, the Society for the Prevention of Cruelty to Animals, and others who periodically write a considerable amount of rubbish on the subject when the newspapers are not feeling well and the gigantic gooseberry season comes in. It may safely be said that were not bearing reins still in use among the ordinary traffic of Piccadilly, Bond Street, Regent Street, etc., the number of accidents as well as the amount of coachbuilders' bills would be largely increased. There is no reason in the world why they can not be put on to be of use when required without causing torture, though no doubt in many cases they are improperly employed. As, however, there are some people—it is doubtful whether they are practical coachmen—who decline to see in bearing reins anything but horrible barbarity, it may not be out of place to state briefly in what cases they may be of some use. Except for the purpose of show, they might be dispensed with for horses in single harness in ninety-nine instances out of a hundred. The hundredth horse might be some heavy-headed boring brute requiring more room in which to be pulled up than is always available in the streets of London. With such a horse a bearing rein, not tighter than is absolutely necessary,

is surely permissible, if only to save the coachman's
arms. It may be granted that bad bitting and worse
driving may have originally conduced to the horse's
mouthless state ; it may also be true that the man
called upon to drive him may not possess the skill of
a Sir St. Vincent Cotton ; but we hold that a proper
use of any mechanical appliance is allowable when
other means fail. The well-meaning faddists who in-
veigh so bitterly against bearing reins are not above
using curb bits ; and, on the whole, horses perhaps
suffer much less from bearing reins than from heavy
hands and curb bits. In double harness, however, the
employment of loose bearing reins has saved many an
accident. If a pair of horses, or four, are driven
straight away for, say, ten miles, baited, and driven
home again, bearing reins are often, it may be ad-
mitted, not wanted ; but it is different with horses
driven in the park and those which have to stand outside shops or private houses while the occupants of the
carriage are shopping or visiting. Horses soon get
warm under the bridle, and when they are pulled up it
is to the moist spot that the flies are attracted ; they
cause a certain amount of irritation, and the horse naturally enough scratches himself, or at least he would
do so had he a hand for the purpose. He drops his
head to the pole, and possibly gets the bit fast. Out
comes the proprietor of the carriage, or perhaps the

policeman on duty appears with a moving-on mission.
The entanglement is not perceived till too late; the
horse does not answer to the reins; a collision occurs,
or perhaps the horse starts kicking and then falls down.
When the evening papers appear, the ubiquitous report-
er will be found to have sent in a paragraph detailing
'a singular carriage accident at the West End.' This is
no fancy sketch, and a bearing rein which is short
enough to prevent such a catastrophe is at the same
time long enough to allow the horse unrestrained freedom of the head. It is the abuse of the bearing reins
(which takes the form of the gag shortened to a cruel
extent), and not the use of them, which merits universal condemnation."

Colonel Hugh Smith Baillie, in his chapter on Hints
to Beginners, in the Badminton Driving, says: "Bearing reins some men write fiercely against. It is the
opinion of many of the best coachmen in England that
a bridle is not complete without a bearing rein. In
my opinion it is wrong to lay down hard-and-fast rules
about bearing reins. I think the gag bearing rein as
screwed up by some London drivers is very bad, and
injurious to the horse; but with kickers the bearing
rein is not only most useful but almost indispensable.
I should very much like to see some of the men who
write so much against bearing reins drive kickers without them; I think they would soon either alter their

opinions or give up driving anything but quiet horses.
I once had the driving for a season of a gray mare, a
determined kicker. She was put into my hands leader
in a team without bearing reins; soon after starting
she put her head down and kicked in a very determined manner, and I had a great difficulty in getting
her head up. I took her out and went to the stable
with a pair, then put a bearing rein on her, and put her
in again. I could then manage her, and drove her for
three months, and a right good one she was. She
kicked occasionally, but I could manage her, which I
could not have done without a bearing rein."

Lord Algernon St. Maur, in his chapter on Single
Harness, in the Badminton Driving, says: " Even in single harness, in all my long forty-mile drives, I always
used a bearing rein, as I found that it steadied a horse;
he looks about him much less, and is not nearly so
likely to rub off his bridle. Those who dislike a bearing rein should buckle the throat lash two or three
holes tighter than usual. Some horses, the moment that
you stop, put down their heads between their fore legs
and try to rub off their bridles—a most dangerous proceeding. All horses look better in a bearing rein when
standing still, as, the moment you stop, down go their
heads, and then a four-hundred-guinea horse looks like
a forty-pounder. In old coaching days I often heard it
said that those coachmen who were the first to take

off the bearing reins were the first to put them on
again. In heavy night coaches, such as the Paul Pry,
which ran from London, through Beaconsfield, to Ox-
ford, weighing about four tons, including passengers
and luggage, and stopped often, running long stages
with underbred horses with hard mouths, bearing
reins were a great safetyguard and assistance both
to the horses and the coachman. One of my
leaders once rubbed his bridle off when stopping
at a shop in a town. Ned Poulter, who at one
time drove the Light Salisbury from Andover to
Basingstoke, in going down a hill near Whitchurch
upset his coach and broke his leg, one of the wheel
horses having caught the crossbar at the bottom of his
bit in the little hook at the end of the pole chain, which
was turned up instead of downward, as it ought to have
been ; the horses became frightened and restive, thus
causing this sad accident. Of course, with nice light-
mouthed horses, when just taking a drive for an hour
or two, all bearing reins can be dispensed with. Bits
are now made without the crossbar at the bottom,
and they are much the safest."

Captain Malet, in his chapter on Coaching on May
Day : Bearing Reins, in Annals of the Road, says :
" On the subject of bearing up coach horses 'The Old
Forester' writes as follows : 'There is no place where
Nimrod is more at home than on the coach box, and

I see with pleasure he has resumed the subject of " the road."

" ' On the subject of " bearing reins " I quite agree with him. It is not only a relief to the arm of the driver, but to the horse himself in a long journey. The look of a thing goes a great way in England, and no man who wishes to turn out well would dispense with the bearing rein. One of your correspondents thinks horses will go safer without the bearing rein, and brings in the Continental practice as proof. I also have been on the Continent a good deal, and have seen the fallacy of that argument. I have also traveled a good deal in mail and fast coaches, and never yet saw a horse fairly down in one of them. I have seen a wheel horse sometimes all but down, and only kept on his legs by a bearing rein.' "

Nimrod, in his chapter on Bearing Reins, Fast Coaches, and Linchpins, in Annals of the Road, says : " I have clearly stated the absolute necessity of bearing up the coach horse, which equally applies to the hand post horse, with only this trifling distinction : the coach horse is generally more above his work than the post horse, and he is also always running home (*ergo*, in a hurry), which is not the case with the post horse. All those who have been accustomed to fast work well know the difficulty of holding horses together and having a perfect command over them even with bearing

reins; but I will venture to add that the man is yet un-
born who could drive some coaches that I could name
without the use of these necessary articles. In the first
place, there are many horses—sometimes whole teams
—that will not face anything but the cheek; and
where is the arm that could bear the weight of four
horses leaning upon it for an hour or more together,
perhaps at full gallop? How much soever humanity
toward horses may be enjoined, regard for our own
species must prevail, and no horse in a coach or a post
chaise is safe without a bearing rein; and for this reason he is in constant danger, from having his head at
liberty, of losing his bridle by rubbing his head against
the pole or against the other horse, and then an accident is almost sure to happen, as was the case with the
York Highflyer coach last year, by which a woman
lost her life. To this must be added the certainty of
his being the more likely to fall, which I have, I think,
clearly proved in a former letter. I know that here
and there is to be found an advocate for no bearing
rein—Mr. Ward, for instance, a good coachman of the
old school, but slow as to pace—and I had a pretty
good taste of it last winter, when staying with Sir Bel-
lingham Graham, in Shropshire. He took it into his
head to drive a pair of wheelers without bearing reins,
and neither the baronet nor myself can soon forget the
strain on the muscles of our arms when driving those

horses, and how glad we were sometimes to change
places. To so experienced a coachman as himself I did
not intrude my opinion, much less attempt to instruct
him ; but had I been the owner of the gallant little
cropped horse that went near-wheel, I would not only
have put a bearing rein upon him, but a good tight side
rein also ; he should have pulled at something else besides my arm. Some people object to side reins upon
a leader, in case of his partner bolting across the road
and taking him with him ; but this can not happen to a
wheeler, as there is the pole and the power of the leaders at the end of it to contend with and to stop him.
There is another reason, and a very strong one, in
favour of the bearing rein. Many horses are good
coach horses for six miles, but far from good ones for
twelve miles. Toward the end of a stage they begin to
bore upon their bits, and were it not for the resistance
of the bearing rein they would get their heads down to
their knees ; and where is the man who could prevent
this being the case with four jaded horses, having
nothing to hang upon but his arms ? "

Lord William Pitt Lennox, in his Coaching, with
Anecdotes of the Road, says : " A fashion has lately
sprung up among us, or rather, I should say, been
adopted (for it is of American origin), and that is,
the almost total abolition of the bearing rein. Much
has been said, written, and argued *pro* and *con*.

Some assert, and with truth, that, generally speaking, it is less safe, for, as the best and soundest horse may once in twelve months make a mistake, the advocates for the loose rein can not help to admit that a bearing rein must assist the horse to recover himself under such circumstances. All extremes are bad, and no one would wish to torture an animal's mouth by pulling his head into an unnatural position, like a dromedary, with an excruciatingly tight bearing rein; but, on the other hand, the absence of one is open to objection. Some horses may and do carry themselves so well that a bearing rein appears superfluous; but, nevertheless, it may be useful, and for this reason should never be entirely dispensed with. I do not say that exceptions may not be permitted. Those possessed of thoroughbred horses, endowed with superior action, may indulge in any whim or caprice they like; and animals worth from four hundred guineas to six hundred guineas apiece, and which go with their heads up, of course do not require a bearing rein, but I condemn the principle for universal adoption; and I have heard the opinions of some of the best coachmen of the day, both amateur and professional, who have asserted that for the generality of horses the practice is a dangerous one. Some animals' heads are put on differently from others, and con-

sequently they vary in their mode of carrying them.
Some, for instance, are stargazers and appear to be
taking lunar observations, while others poke their
heads forward in such a longitudinal form that they
resemble in this particular the Continental swine
trained for grubbing truffles. The plan I should
like to see adopted would be to have a bearing
rein with an elastic end to it, so that the horses
that did not require having their heads held well
up would not be deprived of the ornament of such
a rein; and even with horses that did require it, if
the elastic was pretty strong, it would aid them in
case of a trip or stumble."

C. T. S. Birch Reynardson, in his Down the
Road, says: "Don't think me an old muff, if I say,
Don't drive in London and round the park, where
you no doubt wish to look smart, without bearing
reins. I don't mean to say, Bear your horses up as
if their heads and tails were tied together, but use
bearing reins. Your team will look smarter, and you
will have more comfort with them than without
them. It is very seldom that four horses all carry
their heads in the right place; and if one or two of
them are inclined to get their heads down, it not
only looks bad, but it is a considerable nuisance to
the driver to have to carry his horses' heads, to prevent them lolling them against the pole hook, and

perhaps catching their bits in the pole chains, which I have seen occur more than once. In former days I remember bearing reins on ' the road.' They were discarded, from the fancy, I suppose, that horses worked freer without them. I think they did, but if they got a bit tired, or if they were not of a good sort, they often got their heads down, and lolled about and bored till they made your arms ache."

Athol Maudslay, in his Highways and Horses says: "The celebrated coaching song of the last century was The Tantivy Trot. It ran as follows:

> Here's to the arm that can hold them when gone,
> Still to a gallop inclined, sir;
> Heads in the front, with no bearing reins on,
> Tails with no cruppers behind, sir.

If this was the coaching song of the last century, it only proves that the coachmen of those days had more good sense than is possessed by their grand-children and great-grandchildren, the coachmen of the present day. This verse exactly expresses my own opinion as to bearing reins and cruppers. No bear-ing rein should be used on any account whatever; it is a most abominable practice. A horse, if he be worth anything and has good shoulders, will hold his head well enough without any bearing rein, and the whole position of the animal will be more natu-

ral and more graceful, and he will be less likely
to fall, and, if he does fall, will be better able either
to recover his balance or get up again. A horse,
when he starts a load or mounts a hill, when left to
himself, lowers his head and throws his weight into
the collar; but if his head is held up in the air he
can not employ the same mechanical force. Even on
descending a hill a horse needs the free use of his
head to act as a counterbalance; and it may be re-
marked by anyone who has observed a horse turned
out in a field on the slope of a hill, that, when he
gallops downhill his head is not stuck up in the
air so that he can not see where he is going, but
is held in a natural and suitable position, and one
best qualified to maintain his balance. A horse
when down on the ground always raises his head
before attempting to rise; were his head confined
by a bearing rein when in this position, I doubt if
he could get up at all. A horse is certainly not so
liable to stumble when he has no bearing rein as
when he has one."

CHAPTER XV.

MANY of the carriages illustrated here are of distinctly English origin, and, in consequence, their admirers are charged with Anglomaniacism.

Is it not absurd that persons should exist in this nineteenth century so narrow-minded as to deny the presence of good in anything foreign?

Our English cousins have considered the subject of equipage for years, and have achieved many practical results. England and France have until recently surpassed all other countries in the construction and production of carriages. It is therefore quite right and proper for us to profit as far as possible by their experience, to the extent of reproducing such vehicles as may be useful and practical.

It seems probable that America will before long be foremost in the driving world. Her builders are fully equal, if not superior, to those on the other side of the water. The native woods are the best procurable, and if it were not for the high cost of production the importation of foreign-made carriages would be practically *nil.*

In order to criticise any vehicle impartially, it is necessary to know and understand the uses for which it is intended. The light country station wagon is as much out of place in our city streets as the landau would be if used on some of our sandy country roads.

The excessive weight of English carriages is a subject of comment, and perhaps somewhat justly so in many cases. There is an old saying that "in order to drive handsomely one must drive heavily," and this is pretty generally borne out, provided the word handsomely is properly applied. A young girl in a simple muslin gown may be very *prettily* and *attractively* dressed, oftentimes more so than her sister whose gown is a *handsome* and expensive production from the hands of the celebrated Worth; but while one sister is prepared to attend a formal function, the other is on the way to a small lawn party. Each is therefore appropriately dressed. The handsome gown would look out of place where the pretty one is suitable, and *vice versa*.

The light trotting wagon of purely American origin bears somewhat the same relation to the victoria, for example, as did the sisters' gowns to one another. Each is suited to the purpose for which it is designed: the *handsome* victoria to the formal drive or call, and the *pretty* and *attractive* trotting wagon to a delightful spin on a good boulevard or country road.

A few years ago the supporter of the road wagon made game of the heavier vehicles, and the advocates of the latter type were equally sarcastic. Time has wrought some changes, however, for we find many men of means and taste indulging in both the heavy and light harness types, keeping each class distinct and yet turning both out well. To such an end as this the present work is directed. If more vehicles of the heavier type are illustrated, it is simply because there happen to be more standard carriages of that sort in general use.

Weight, by the way, in a carriage does not necessarily mean a heavy draught where the roads are good, for a heavily loaded four-in-hand coach, well constructed, will run with comparatively little exertion on the part of the horses.

The side-bar wagon is one of the few examples of a standard vehicle which is peculiarly identified with this country. For a quarter of a century it has changed very little in general shape, and is not likely to do so for some time to come. Fashion at one time dictated that the lining should be green and the tops have three bows ; at another, blue with four bows, etc. To-day the design of the vehicle is almost unvarying, but each owner exercises his individual taste as to colours and trimming, which is much the more rational principle.

The reason for this consistency is found in the practicality of the road wagon for its purpose, combining, as it does lightness, strength, and a shape which is in keeping with the swinging stride of the trotter pure and simple.

A number of heavier carriages have become standard in much the same manner, and a rapid departure from the designs which have been in use for many years is generally unsuccessful. The introduction of an entirely new vehicle is sometimes a benefit, more frequently a detriment.

Almost every enthusiastic owner in the early part of his career is seized with invention in the embryo state, and is not satisfied until he has evolved some abortion in the way of a carriage *which shall be noticed.* He generally succeeds in achieving this end, and presents his production to the view of his unfortunate friends with the air of a conqueror. Unless he is a crank, however, he will appreciate the error of his ways within a few years, and will hide his diminished head when the subject of his chef d'œuvre is mentioned.

Any changes in existing designs of carriages which give more symmetry of outline or improvement in construction should be welcomed. A close observer will note that such improvements are quite often brought about by *simplification,* but very rarely by *elaboration.*

Take, for example, the "sedan" broughams and the cabriolets which have been introduced within the past few years, and are what might be termed elaborations of standard carriages; even the casual observer realizes that these carriages must be relegated to the hack stands long before their period of usefulness is accomplished, the only question being whether the hackmen will have them at any price.

The more eccentric the type, the shorter lived it is and the sooner it must be supplanted. This quality is just what is wanted by our rapidly growing class of nouveaux riches. They wish their acquaintances to know that *they* buy a new carriage every year, so the more noticeable the change the better they are suited. Who can blame the coachbuilders for catering to this class, who form really their best-paying patrons?

It quite often happens that there are several existing designs of the same variety of carriage, all of which may be equally correct. In a proper carriage of any sort we will find the following points: Appropriate dignity with simplicity, well-balanced lines, an absence of elaborate and fancy carving or iron work, and an air of luxury without ostentation.

Such an effect can only be produced when the proportions and treatment throughout are in perfect accord—an end much more difficult of attainment than one would at first suppose.

CARRIAGES FOR AN OWNER'S DRIVING.

FOUR–WHEELERS.

We will now take up the leading types of four-wheel carriages which are intended for an owner's individual driving.

Mail Phaëton.

The mail phaëton (Plate LXI) heads the list of such carriages, and is and has been for many years the highest type of vehicle for the purpose. It was first introduced early in the time of George IV as a vehicle for city use, and later was employed extensively in making long journeys. It is capacious and thoroughly comfortable, hanging, as it does, on leather robbins with platform springs, and is undoubtedly the most luxurious carriage of its kind in existence. It is properly a very large vehicle, and requires horses measuring sixteen hands or over, with a great deal of quality and good level action, which can do at least twelve miles an hour. For driving in the park two servants should be carried, both, properly speaking, in grooms' liveries. This carriage, being one of the most dignified in type, must never be turned out carelessly. The harness is much the same as that for the four-in-hand park wheel, and requires in town the use of full bearing reins

Plate LXI: Mail Phaëton "Turned Out."

Plate LXII: Rear View of Mail Phaëton.

Plate LXIII: Demi-Mail Phaëton.

Plate LXIV · *Stanhope Phaëton.*

and Buxton bits, also loin straps. Considered from another point of view—viz., as a travelling carriage, with either two or three horses abreast, road harness, and servants in stable clothes—it is one of the most suitable carriages possible. The hood, which is ample, provides a thorough protection in stormy weather, and there is sufficient room for the stowage of luggage, etc., especially when the hind panel is hinged.

Demi-mail Phaëton.

Next to the mail in order of dignity comes the demi-mail phaëton (Plate LXIII). In this carriage the perch has been dispensed with, and it is a trifle lighter and smaller throughout; it requires the services of only one groom. The horses should be of the same stamp as those used in the mail, but smaller and with more brilliant action.

Stanhope Phaëton.

Next in order comes the Stanhope phaëton (Plate LXIV), which was originally produced by mounting a Stanhope gig on four wheels and adding thereto a boot for the servant. It is smaller than either the mail or demi-mail, and has an arch which admits of the front wheels turning under. It may, if desired, be used with one horse.

T-Cart.

The T-cart is in reality only a modification of the Stanhope phaëton, without the hood and with a few other trifling differences in detail.

Spider Phaëton.

The spider phaëton (Plate LXV), which comes last on this list, is a more modern introduction, and is really one of the smartest types for the young man's driving. It should be brilliantly horsed; animals about fifteen two hands in height, lightly built, with a great deal of quality and as much all-around action as can be produced, provided it is progressive, are what is required. This carriage is especially useful for horse show work, as it is light enough to enable the horses to do themselves justice.

Four-wheeled Dogcart or Gamecart.

This carriage is a smart example of its type, and may be used either tandem or with a pair.

It will be noticed that the lamps used on all these carriages have dark shutters, so that they can with perfect propriety be carried in the daytime. The spider phaëton illustrated here is, however, an exception, and a lamp such as is shown should be dispensed with for

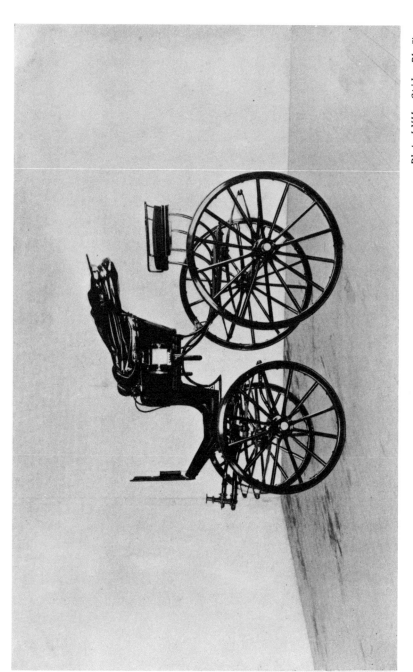

Plate LXV: Spider Phaëton.

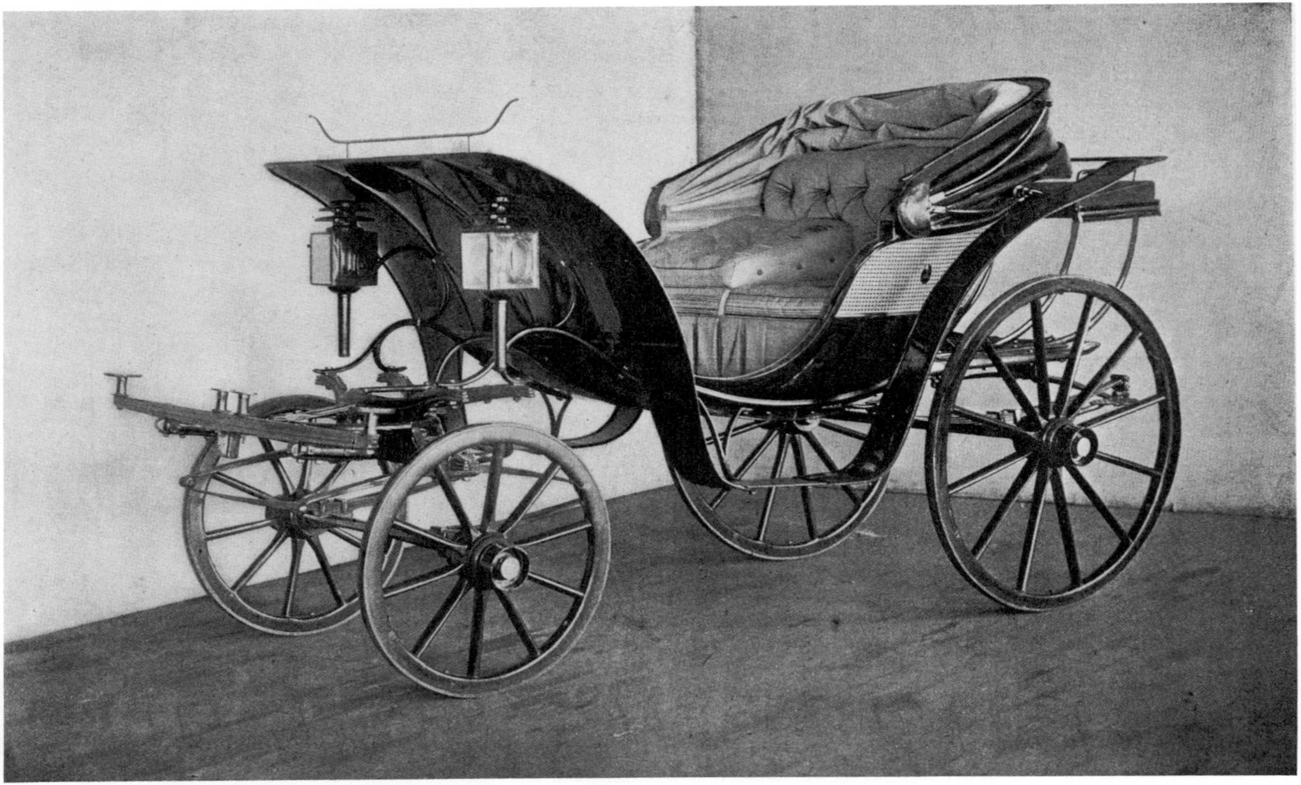

Plate LXVI: George IV Phaëton.

day driving. The small plain square lamp might, however, be carried in place at all times.

Having discussed the carriages appropriate to a gentleman's driving, we will next consider those suitable for a lady's use. The field in this instance is a very narrow one, and in consequence a great many women have been inclined to affect the driving of a man's carriage.

George IV Phaëton.

The George IV phaëton (Plate LXVI) heads the list, and is the most dignified of all carriages for ladies' driving. It is thoroughly luxurious in outline, and demands the smartest possible turning out. No vehicle is better suited to display a fashionable costume. A well-dressed woman driving a brilliant, well-mannered, and nicely rounded pair of matched horses, and attended by a single groom in immaculate livery, either a tidy lad or an older man who is slight and short, presents a most charming picture.

Peter's Ladies' Phaëton.

Next in order comes a carriage which is known as the Peter's ladies' phaëton (Plate LXVII), being a copy of one originally built by an English coachbuilder of the name. It is an attractive carriage, and somewhat lighter than the one last mentioned; is also better adapted to morning and informal use than the George IV, and is generally drawn by ponies from fourteen three to fifteen hands high.

While there are several other phaëtons for ladies' use, there seem to be none suited to park work, and which may be considered standard, except these two.

It may be well to state in connection with the full mail and George IV phaëtons, that they are very expensive carriages, and there being comparatively few persons owning stables which would admit of their use, they will be found difficult to dispose of except at a very great sacrifice. Such, in fact, is the case with most of the carriages which require a treatment out of the general run in order to turn them out successfully.

TWO-WHEELERS.

Under this heading are given photographs of some of the best types of two-wheeled vehicles intended for single-horse driving by an owner.

Tilbury.

The tilbury (Plates LXIX and LXX) was originally designed by the Hon. Fitzroy Stanhope, and built by a coachbuilder named Tilbury. It is one of the oldest and handsomest two-wheelers in use at the present

Plate LXVII: Peter's Lady's Phaëton.

Plate LXVIII : Four-wheeled Dogcart

Plate LXIX: Tilbury (Side View).

Plate LXX · Tilbury (Rear View)

Plate LXXI: Stanhope Gig.

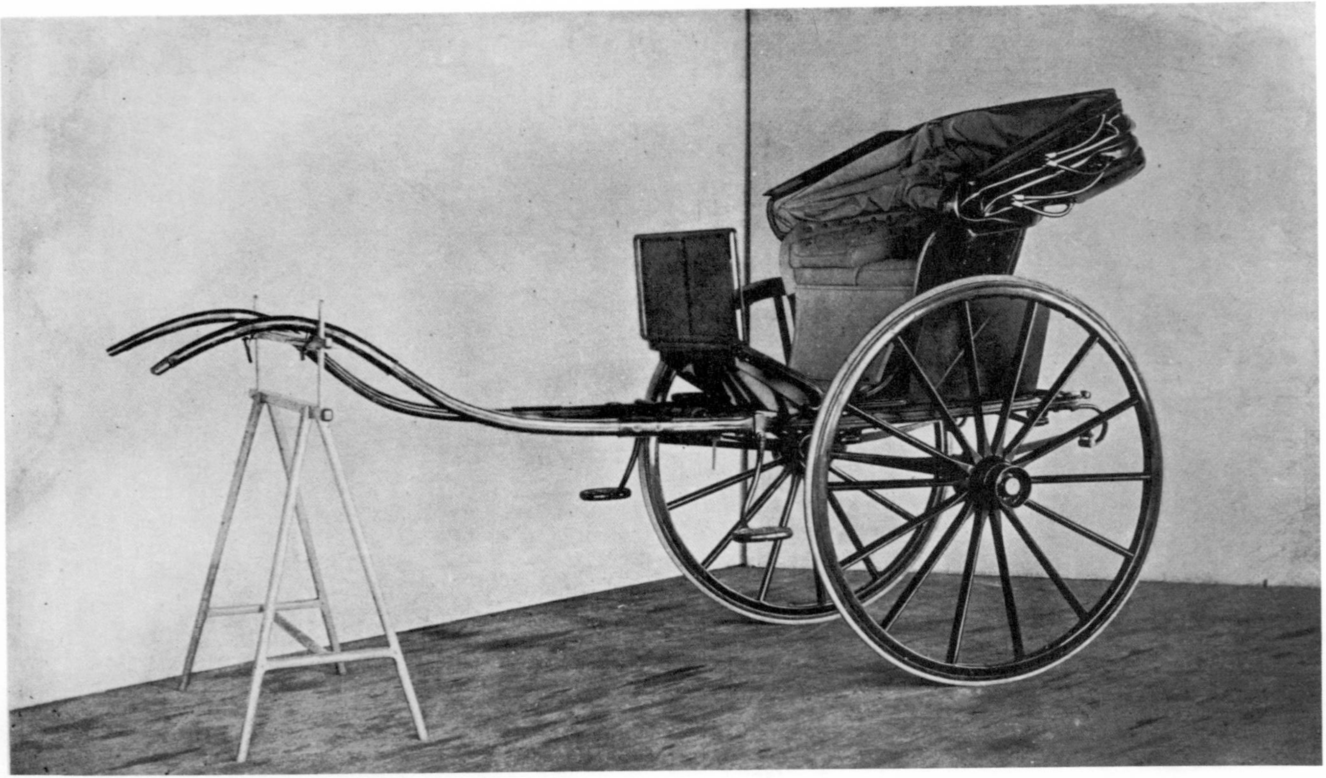

Plate LXXII: Hooded Gig or Buggy.

time. Unfortunately, for many years it was laid aside, but it has recently been resurrected, and there is no carriage more smart for use with a brilliant goer. The illustrations show both its side and rear views, which seemed necessary in order to exhibit its characteristics in detail. This requires the gig harness, as, in fact, do all the carriages mentioned in the following list, except possibly the skeleton gig.

Stanhope Gig.

Next in order comes the Stanhope gig (Plate LXXI), also designed by the Hon. Fitzroy Stanhope, and on the insistence of Mr. Tilbury it was given his name. The carriage has held its own ever since those early days about the year 1815, and, although not quite as generally used at the present time, always will look proper.

Hooded Gig.

The hooded gig (Plate LXXII) is a dignified vehicle, being practically a Stanhope gig with hood attached.

Park Gate Gig.

The "park gate" gig (Plate LXXIII) is a copy from an old print, and is a very smart vehicle, especially adapted to the small, thickset hackney type of horse.

Very Spicy Gig.

The "very spicy" gig (Plate LXXIV) is another departure from an old print, which is a slight modification of the tilbury and also a very smart vehicle. Like the tilbury, it is particularly suited to a light, airy-going type of horse.

By the way, one can grasp to a certain extent, from the outlines of the carriage itself the stamp of horse which it requires. In all these carriages the servant, when carried, should be a smart, dapper, young, top-booted groom, who should sit beside his his master with his arms folded.

Skeleton Gig.

The skeleton gig (Plate LXXV) is a modification of a vehicle built contemporaneously with the tilbury and Stanhope. It is a very useful carriage, and on account of its lightness is especially adapted to exercising; it therefore requires a sporting harness, and may be driven by a servant in stable clothes.

It will be noticed that the lamps on all these carriages are very simple and plain, and can with perfect propriety be carried at all times. Lazy coachmen are fond of using rubber covers for their lamps in stormy weather; these should, under no circumstances, be permitted.

Plate LXXIII: "Park Gate" Gig.

Plate LXXIV : "Very Spicy" Gig.

Plate LXXV : Skeleton Gig.

Plate LXXVII : Village Cart.

Plate LXXVIII : High Skeleton Gig.

Paris Lady's Chaise.

The Paris lady's chaise (Plate LXXVI) is a vehicle of French introduction intended for a lady's use. It does not admit of the carrying of a servant, and requires a well-rounded horse a trifle over fifteen hands, rather of the hackney stamp.

The Curricle.

The curricle (Plate LXXIX) was for years one of the most fashionable town carriages, and is in many respects similar to its successor, the cabriolet, although the latter is drawn by a single horse and the former by a pair. Sidney, in his Book of the Horse, gives a very good illustration of the curricle as turned out in the days of Charles Dickens. This was the carriage which many of Miss Austen's heroes were supposed to have affected. It is described as being "drawn by a pair of horses perfectly matched in size, colour, quality, and step; the harness being profusely decorated with silver ornaments, united by a silver bar, which supported a silver-mounted pole; preceded or followed by two grooms mounted on another pair of horses equally well matched with the first, secured the driver and his companion a superb effect, which combined the maximum of expense with the minimum of convenience." Such a carriage should be turned out to-day in a very much more simple style, and is the best adapted for use with a pair of any two-wheeled vehicle.

The Cabriolet.

The cabriolet (Plate LXXX) is described by S. Sidney as being "a curricle with a pair of shafts and without the groom's rumble. It was in the height of fashion in the earlier days of Queen Victoria's reign."

The cabriolet requires a single horse of great size and beauty, with extraordinary action, especially in his slow paces. The groom, who stands behind, is so small as to be of little use save for effect.

The horse shown in the plate more nearly approaches the ideal than almost any other animal in this country, combining, as he does, marvellous action at both slow and fast paces with great size, quality, and unusual beauty of form.

NON-SPORTING TWO-WHEELERS.

The Hansom Cab.

The hansom cab (Plates LXXXI and LXXXII) as stated in Sidney's Book of the Horse, was invented by a Mr. Hansom, architect of the Birmingham Town Hall, and apparently came into use about the year

Plate LXXX: Cabriolet "Turned Out."

Plate LXXXI: Hansom Cab.

Plate LXXXII : Hansom Cab.

Plate LXXXIII : Breaking Cart and Harness.

Plate LXXXIV : Jaunting Car.

1840. It is essentially a man's carriage for town use, and in a city where good paving exists will be found very satisfactory. It has an unostentatious look when the servant is dressed in either stable clothes or a plain black cutaway coat, top felt hat, with breeches and gaiters. In rainy weather he is supplied with what is called an upper benjamin, as shown in Plate LXXXII. This garment is made of a waterproof material, and is very similar in cut to those used by four-horse coachmen. The hansom-cab horse should always have considerable quality and good level action, for much of the smooth riding of the cab depends on the action of the horse, provided he is properly harnessed.

Breaking Cart.

Plate LXXXIII shows a useful breaking cart and harness. Both are thoroughly adapted to the purpose for which they are intended.

It will be noticed that the harness is strongly but simply made, and the shafts long enough to keep the horse well clear of the dash.

The Jaunting Car.

Plate LXXXIV is an illustration of a jaunting car which is used in Ireland, and is considered by some persons a useful and practical vehicle.

NON-SPORTING FOUR-WHEELERS.

The Brougham.

This carriage is the most practical and the most generally used of all town carriages. It is the only closed carriage which looks well with one horse and one servant, and when turned out with a pair of horses of a suitable size, with either one or two servants, it may be made to look really smart.

Invented, as it was, in 1839 by Lord Chancellor Brougham, from whom its name was derived, it has been ever since that time the one carriage patronized by all conditions of men and women, because of its usefulness and effect.

The early broughams were built to hold two persons only, and were afterward extended to accommodate four. At the present day the brougham for two passengers is the most generally used and is the best in appearance; but the so-called extension brougham is perfectly correct and a useful carriage, especially where there is a family of children.

As S. Sidney says, in chronicling their history: " They rapidly came into use in the highest circles, when the fairest of the fair discovered that the windows presented charming portraits, and that, low hung on wheels, they had all the advantages of the curricle

Plate LXXXV : Lady's Brougham.

Plate LXXXVI: Bachelor's Brougham.

Plate LXXXVII: Rear View of Brougham.

Plate LXXXVIII · Brougham

Plate LXXXIX: A Modern Brougham.

Plate XC: *Brougham*
(Front and Rear View)

or cabriolet, with none of their dangers or difficulties. It was found that the magnificent class of horse previously appropriated to the cabriolet looked twice as well in a brougham, could travel twice as far, and, with a weight off his fore legs, last twice as long. Besides, if it were necessary to make a long journey instead of a succession of flashes through street or park, the brougham became the most agreeable conveyance where the beauties of Nature were not the object of the journey."

In England it has been the practice for many years to use the brougham for service in the country, and where the roads will admit of so heavy a carriage it is a most desirable vehicle. Rubber tires add greatly to their comfort in the city, and are one of the most practical improvements of modern times.

Plate LXXXV shows a lady's brougham which won in an appointment class in Madison Square Garden. The details throughout are excellent. The lady's brougham requires two servants when drawn by a pair. To carry out the full idea, these servants should be trim, dapper, and not too tall, the groom being a trifle the smaller and shorter. Plate LXXXVII shows the rear view of the servants on the brougham. It will be noticed that the groom sits a little lower than the coachman. It does not look well to have the groom or footman show more height on the box than the

coachman. The cushion for the driving seat is made
on the same level for both servants, and is either
tufted or finished plain, slanting slightly toward the
front, but not so much as to prevent the servants sitting squarely and comfortably on it. Nothing looks
worse than to see a coachman with his legs stretched
out in front of him; and there is no position more
conducive to heavy hands.

The bachelor brougham (Plate LXXXVI), it will be
noticed, is turned out with one servant, and loin straps
are dispensed with, otherwise there is very little difference in the general treatment. The painting may,
however, be of brighter colours than in the lady's
brougham.

Where there are two servants on a brougham, the
stable shutters should be up when the carriage is driven
from the stable to the door, on reaching which they
should immediately be lowered by the groom or footman and the windows raised halfway. This practice
should be pursued whenever the carriage is driven any
distance without occupants.

It seems to be the general impression, in order to
properly distinguish the bachelor's brougham from the
lady's in horse-show appointment classes, that a cargo
of miscellaneous masculinities or femininities must be
carried, but this is not at all essential.

So-called Cabriolet (Plate XCI.)

The name cabriolet belongs properly to the two-wheeled carriage much used in England in days gone by, and shown in Plate LXXX.

For some unknown reason the term cabriolet has been applied by our carriagebuilders in recent years to a carriage which one might term a modification of the victoria. This carriage, although lacking the dignity and grace of the victoria, is a practical one, as it admits of turning out with the simplicity of the brougham, and can therefore very properly be used by a woman for shopping, etc., when she wishes to be out in the open air.

The whole treatment with regard to harness and appointments is identical with that of the brougham. The carriage shown happens to be lined with a light material, which is to a great extent a matter of taste. Plain morocco simply and practically fastened is, however, most to be recommended for both these carriages.

It may be said that a miniature eight or "C" spring victoria turned out in the same manner is handsomer, more comfortable, and equally appropriate.

The Landau (*Plate XCII*).

Next to the brougham as a useful carriage for family purposes the landau should be mentioned, for it is the most practical city carriage extant for four passengers.

In ordinary stables it is well to have this carriage built somewhat in miniature, for this admits of using the same harness, general appointments, etc., as are required on a full-sized brougham. But when the full-sized landau is used, the horses, harness, servants, etc., should correspond with those described for the chariot d'Orsay.

Eight or "C" Spring Victoria (*Plate XCIII*).

This carriage is an adaptation of the old cabriolet phaëton, and first came into use as a fashionable one during the French empire. It belongs properly to the class of "grand carriages," and should be used only for formal calls or for the "promenade on wheels." When full sized it requires a pair of horses over sixteen hands high, perfectly matched, and with much quality and action. The harness admits of a little more elaboration than that of the brougham, bottle-shaped pads being the more correct. The horses' tails should be a trifle set up, and either banged so that they hang

Plate XCI : "*So-called*" *Cabriolet*
"*Turned Out.*"

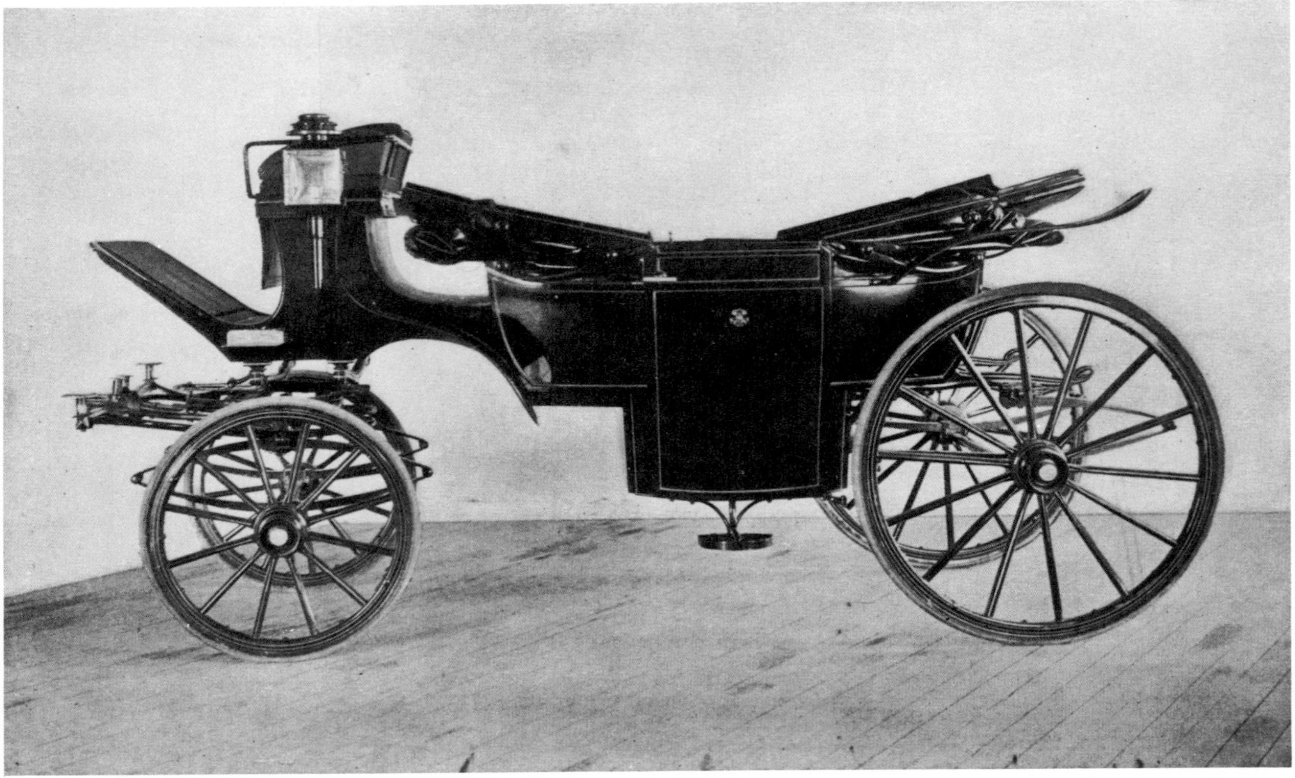

Plate XCII: Landau.

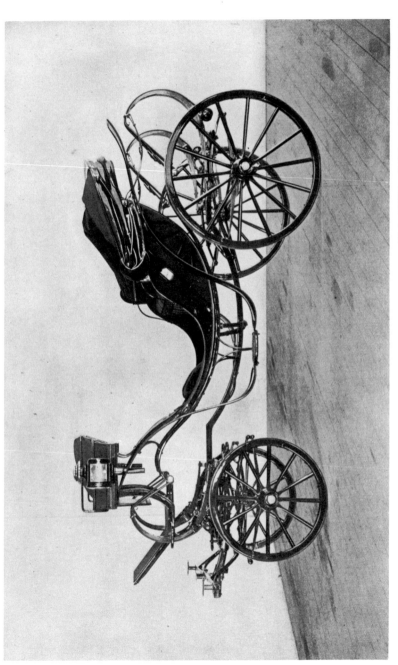

Plate XCIII: "C" or Eight Spring Victoria.

Plate XCIV : *Coupé d'Orsay.*

gracefully about to the top of the second thigh, or pulled so that they do not come below the traces.

The coachman, on all of these grand carriages, should be a large man, somewhat portly, and custom up to the present time advocates his sitting on a raised box. This custom, however, is subject to criticism, for the coachman and footman, sitting, as they do, on such different levels, detract in a measure from the balanced appearance of the equipage. It is to be hoped that a few years' time will show an absence of the driving cushion, even on vehicles of this type.

The footman should be tall and slim, and should be thoroughly well trained. Dummy box coats should never be used, and, ordinarily speaking it is best not to show the servants' greatcoats, unless it is absolutely necessary that they be carried on account of the weather.

Coupé d'Orsay (Plate XCIV).

This carriage is the French adaptation of the chariot d'Orsay, and while not quite as dignified as the latter carriage, it is nevertheless a formal one and not intended for everyday use.

It should be horsed and harnessed as described for the "C" spring victoria.

The Calèche (*Plate XCV*).

This carriage can be classed, as is the chariot d'Orsay, under the heading of "state" in the turning out, as it corresponds in all points with that of the carriage just mentioned.

The example here shown is a most excellent one, for it will be noticed that, although in itself an elaborate carriage, it has no unnecessary decoration, and its lines throughout are easy and graceful.

The Chariot d'Orsay (*Plate XCVI*).

Here we have a grand carriage which properly belongs to the "state" order. It is not at all suited for use in this democratic country of ours, unless the stable be supplied with a brougham as well. It is intended simply for the most formal calling or for the park.

The general appointments are similar to those of the "C" spring victoria, except that the horses should have more substance, and should wear breechings.

In England, where this carriage can be turned out with servants in powdered wigs and smallclothes, it is customary to use hammercloths and a knife-board for the footmen, but even there less ostentation is seen to-day than in the past.

Plate XCV : Calèche.

Plate XCVI: Chariot d'Orsay.

Plate XCVII: Landau Grande Daumont.

Plate XCVIII : Omnibus.

The example shown here would conform more thoroughly to the general idea of the vehicle if supplied with Collinge's in place of mail axles.

Landau Grande Daumont (Plate XCVII).

The equipage shown here is as turned out in the days of the Empire, and is a most excellent example of a "state" carriage. Those interested in appointments will notice how perfectly all the details correspond with those which are proper at the present day. Of course, the whole establishment is more ostentatious than is admissible in this country, but such a carriage, with a boot and coachman's box, splendidly horsed and turned out as described for the chariot d'Orsay, could be used here with perfect propriety.

The Omnibus (Plates XCVIII and XCIX).

This carriage is of French origin, and has come into general use comparatively recently. It may fairly be called the most useful all-around vehicle we have, and in a good-sized family stable can scarcely be dispensed with.

The accompanying illustrations portray one of the best designs of the genus omnibus which we have in this country, and it is well turned out. The absence of loin straps and the use of Liverpool bits may be

criticised by some, but it should be borne in mind
that the omnibus classes rather as an informal carriage, and its treatment admits of a slight relaxa-
tion from the most rigid rules of form.

In the morning the omnibus is used for station
work, etc., in the country; and in town, to take the
nurses and children for an airing. In the first instance it is proper for the servants to wear their
undress liveries (described in Chapter X), and the same
dress is preferable in the second instance. When this
carriage is used in the afternoon or evening, either
in town or at a fashionable watering place, the servants should wear their full liveries, as in the photograph, and the harness should carry out the same
idea. For real country use, undress liveries at all
times are in the best taste.

It is customary to have a roof seat on such an
omnibus, the lazyback and cushion for which are
removed when the servant is to drive, except when
the seat is needed for the transporting of house servants. This seat is ordinarily used when the carriage
is temporarily transformed into a four-in-hand trap.
The servants then wear undress liveries and ride
inside, while the owner and his guests occupy the box
and roof seats.

It must be remembered that the omnibus hardly
classes as a proper four-in-hand vehicle, and for this

Plate XCIX: Omnibus "Turned Out."

Plate C: Hungarian Phaëton.

Plate CI: Modern Trotting Sulky with Pneumatic Tires.

*Plate CII : Skeleton Wagon
with Pneumatic Tires.*

Plate CIII: Single Roadster.

Plate CIV: Road Pair "Turned Out."

Plate CV : Side-Bar Road Wagon.

Plate CVI: Road Wagons
(Front and Rear View)

Plate CVII: Light Four-wheeled Dogcart
(Side Bar).

Plate CVIII : Surrey.

Plate CIX: Lady's Phaëton.

Plate CX: *Extension Top Phaëton.*

reason it should be turned out as plainly as possible to avoid criticism.

Pole chains should be used in place of pole pieces, and the lamps should be carried inside.

For country use, where it is often necessary to drive long distances over heavy roads, an adjustment of two poles, so that three horses can be driven abreast, is very practical.

The baggage rail on the roof adds greatly to the usefulness of the carriage, as it enables one frequently to dispense with the services of a baggage wagon.

Hungarian Phaëton (Plate C).

Up to the present time this carriage has not been used in America, but it is so attractive in design that we have illustrated it, thinking it might find some admirer who would care to have it reproduced.

CARRIAGES OF AMERICAN ORIGIN.

Road Wagon.

The road wagon (Plate CV), light four-wheeled dog-cart (Plate CVII), surrey (Plate CVIII), and possibly the lady's phaëton (Plate CIX) and extension top phaëton (Plate CX), are properly turned out with trotting-

bred horses with tails undocked, and with that beauti-
ful production of our harnessmakers' art, the road
harness. These carriages are most useful for country
work, and for fast trotting generally. The servant,
when carried, should always wear undress livery.

Six-seat Rockaway.

The six-seat rockaway (Plate CXI) and coupé rockaway (Plate CXII) are familiar to all, but have been,
more or less of necessity, relegated to country use, as
it is difficult for a coachman to drive in our crowded
city streets from such a low seat. The general appointments described for the brougham are in order for use
in these carriages.

Wagonette and Station Wagon.

The wagonette (Plates CXIII and CXIV) and station
wagon (Plate CXV) are still further evidences of American practicality. The wagonette especially is a vehicle
which can scarcely be dispensed with in the country
for running to the station, etc., as it carries the largest
possible number of passengers with the least effort to
the horses. Undress liveries should almost invariably
be used on such carriages, and a brougham harness
is proper ; but where the harness is made solely for
this purpose, it should be a trifle lighter throughout
than that for the brougham. Roominess is one of the

Plate CXI: Six-Seat Rockaway.

Plate CXIII: Wagonette.

Plate CXIV : Wagonette with Pair.

Plate CXV : Depot Wagon.

Plate CXVI: Runabout "Turned Out."

Plate CXVII : Buckboard.

Plate CXVIII: Errand Wagon.

most important features of the station wagon, and it
is particularly necessary to have the door sufficiently
wide, and so arranged that when the curtains are
down there is room for a woman to get in and out
comfortably without soiling her gown against the
wheels. There is no stereotyped pattern for these carriages, as practicality is the most important point to
be considered, and many persons differ as to what con-
stitutes this.

Runabout.

The runabout (Plate CXVI) and buckboard (Plate
CXVII) are also most useful vehicles. The former to-
day may be said to be more generally used than any
other light wagon for two passengers. The harness
which looks best and is most generally used is described in the chapter on Harness and Harnessing; but
where the horse is a long-tailed roadster an American
trotting harness should be used.

Errand Wagon.

We have given in Plate CXVIII an example of
a practical business wagon for running on errands,
station work, etc.

NONDESCRIPT CARRIAGES.

There are several carriages, such as the slat-side phaëton and beach phaëton here shown, which may fairly be classed under this head. They are modifications of carriages which are used on the other side of the water, and are better adapted to our use when of light construction, although they lose somewhat of their character. Of course there are many other carriages which may come under the same designation, some good, many bad.

Undress liveries should be used with almost all of them.

THE END.

Plate CXIX : Four-Seat Slat-Side Phaëton.

Plate CXX : Six-Seat Slat-Side Phaëton.

Plate CXXI: Six-Seat
Beach or Hunting Phaëton

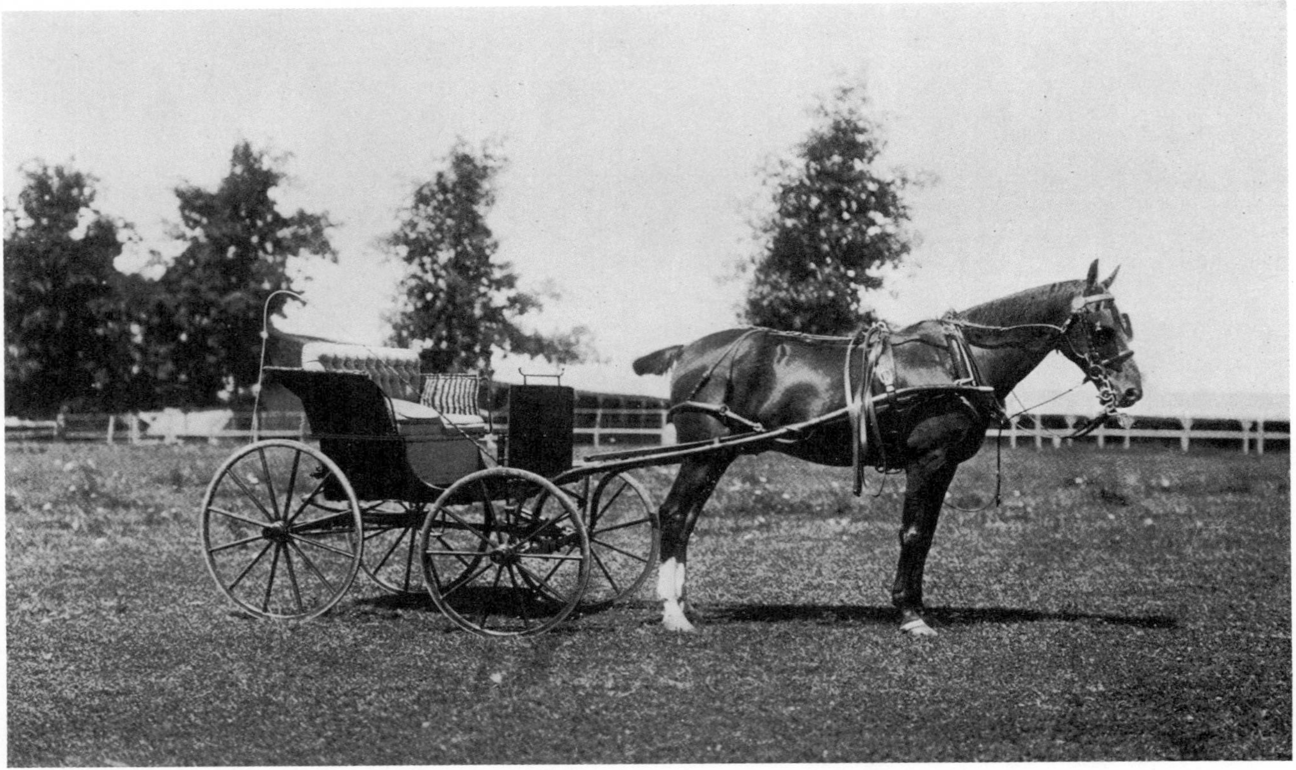

Plate CXXII: A Smart

Plate CXXIII : Vis-à-vis.

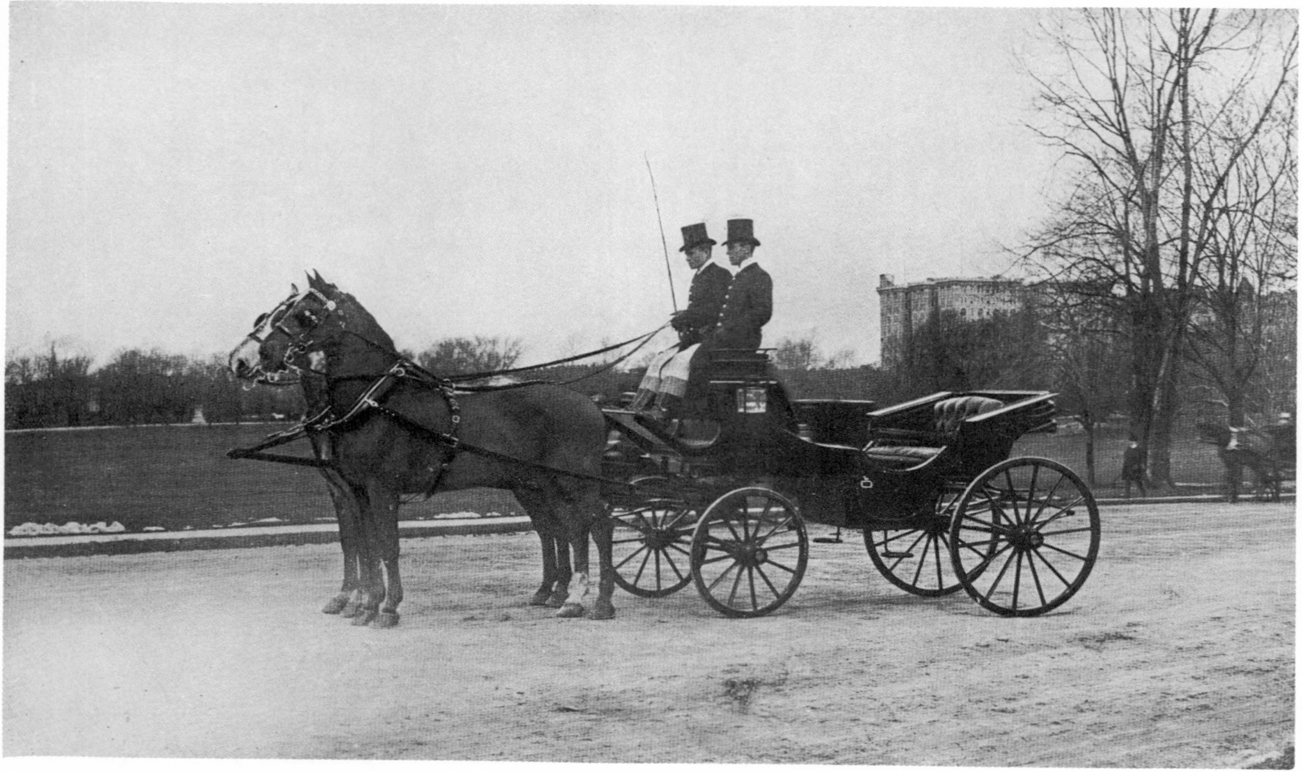

Plate CXXIV: Vis-à-vis

A CATALOG OF SELECTED
DOVER BOOKS
IN ALL FIELDS OF INTEREST

A CATALOG OF SELECTED
DOVER BOOKS
IN ALL FIELDS OF INTEREST

DRAWINGS OF REMBRANDT, edited by Seymour Slive. Updated Lippmann, Hofstede de Groot edition, with definitive scholarly apparatus. All portraits, biblical sketches, landscapes, nudes. Oriental figures, classical studies, together with selection of work by followers. 550 illustrations. Total of 630pp. 9⅛ × 12¼.
21485-0, 21486-9 Pa., Two-vol. set $29.90

GHOST AND HORROR STORIES OF AMBROSE BIERCE, Ambrose Bierce. 24 tales vividly imagined, strangely prophetic, and decades ahead of their time in technical skill: "The Damned Thing," "An Inhabitant of Carcosa," "The Eyes of the Panther," "Moxon's Master," and 20 more. 199pp. 5⅜ × 8½. 20767-6 Pa. $4.95

ETHICAL WRITINGS OF MAIMONIDES, Maimonides. Most significant ethical works of great medieval sage, newly translated for utmost precision, readability. Laws Concerning Character Traits, Eight Chapters, more. 192pp. 5⅜ × 8½.
24522-5 Pa. $5.95

THE EXPLORATION OF THE COLORADO RIVER AND ITS CANYONS, J. W. Powell. Full text of Powell's 1,000-mile expedition down the fabled Colorado in 1869. Superb account of terrain, geology, vegetation, Indians, famine, mutiny, treacherous rapids, mighty canyons, during exploration of last unknown part of continental U.S. 400pp. 5⅜ × 8½. 20094-9 Pa. $8.95

HISTORY OF PHILOSOPHY, Julián Marías. Clearest one-volume history on the market. Every major philosopher and dozens of others, to Existentialism and later. 505pp. 5⅜ × 8½. 21739-6 Pa. $9.95

ALL ABOUT LIGHTNING, Martin A. Uman. Highly readable nontechnical survey of nature and causes of lightning, thunderstorms, ball lightning, St. Elmo's Fire, much more. Illustrated. 192pp. 5⅜ × 8½. 25237-X Pa. $5.95

SAILING ALONE AROUND THE WORLD, Captain Joshua Slocum. First man to sail around the world, alone, in small boat. One of great feats of seamanship told in delightful manner. 67 illustrations. 294pp. 5⅜ × 8½. 20326-3 Pa. $4.95

LETTERS AND NOTES ON THE MANNERS, CUSTOMS AND CONDITIONS OF THE NORTH AMERICAN INDIANS, George Catlin. Classic account of life among Plains Indians: ceremonies, hunt, warfare, etc. 312 plates. 572pp. of text. 6⅛ × 9¼. 22118-0, 22119-9, Pa., Two-vol. set $17.90

THE SECRET LIFE OF SALVADOR DALÍ, Salvador Dalí. Outrageous but fascinating autobiography through Dalí's thirties with scores of drawings and sketches and 80 photographs. A must for lovers of 20th-century art. 432pp. 6½ × 9¼. (Available in U.S. only) 27454-3 Pa. $9.95

CATALOG OF DOVER BOOKS

AMERICAN CLIPPER SHIPS: 1833–1858, Octavius T. Howe & Frederick C. Matthews. Fully-illustrated, encyclopedic review of 352 clipper ships from the period of America's greatest maritime supremacy. Introduction. 109 halftones. 5 black-and-white line illustrations. Index. Total of 928pp. 5⅜ × 8½.
25115-2, 25116-0 Pa., Two-vol. set $21.90

TOWARDS A NEW ARCHITECTURE, Le Corbusier. Pioneering manifesto by great architect, near legendary founder of "International School." Technical and aesthetic theories, views on industry, economics, relation of form to function, "mass-production spirit," much more. Profusely illustrated. Unabridged translation of 13th French edition. Introduction by Frederick Etchells. 320pp. 6⅛ × 9¼. (Available in U.S. only)
25023-7 Pa. $8.95

THE BOOK OF KELLS, edited by Blanche Cirker. Inexpensive collection of 32 full-color, full-page plates from the greatest illuminated manuscript of the Middle Ages, painstakingly reproduced from rare facsimile edition. Publisher's Note. Captions. 32pp. 9⅜ × 12¼. (Available in U.S. only)
24345-1 Pa. $5.95

BEST SCIENCE FICTION STORIES OF H. G. WELLS, H. G. Wells. Full novel *The Invisible Man,* plus 17 short stories: "The Crystal Egg," "Aepyornis Island," "The Strange Orchid," etc. 303pp. 5⅜ × 8½. (Available in U.S. only)
21531-8 Pa. $6.95

AMERICAN SAILING SHIPS: Their Plans and History, Charles G. Davis. Photos, construction details of schooners, frigates, clippers, other sailcraft of 18th to early 20th centuries—plus entertaining discourse on design, rigging, nautical lore, much more. 137 black-and-white illustrations. 240pp. 6⅛ × 9¼.
24658-2 Pa. $6.95

ENTERTAINING MATHEMATICAL PUZZLES, Martin Gardner. Selection of author's favorite conundrums involving arithmetic, money, speed, etc., with lively commentary. Complete solutions. 112pp. 5⅜ × 8½.
25211-6 Pa. $3.95

THE WILL TO BELIEVE, HUMAN IMMORTALITY, William James. Two books bound together. Effect of irrational on logical, and arguments for human immortality. 402pp. 5⅜ × 8½.
20291-7 Pa. $8.95

THE HAUNTED MONASTERY and THE CHINESE MAZE MURDERS, Robert Van Gulik. 2 full novels by Van Gulik continue adventures of Judge Dee and his companions. An evil Taoist monastery, seemingly supernatural events; overgrown topiary maze that hides strange crimes. Set in 7th-century China. 27 illustrations. 328pp. 5⅜ × 8½.
23502-5 Pa. $6.95

CELEBRATED CASES OF JUDGE DEE (DEE GOONG AN), translated by Robert Van Gulik. Authentic 18th-century Chinese detective novel; Dee and associates solve three interlocked cases. Led to Van Gulik's own stories with same characters. Extensive introduction. 9 illustrations. 237pp. 5⅜ × 8½.
23337-5 Pa. $5.95

Prices subject to change without notice.

Available at your book dealer or write for free catalog to Dept. GI, Dover Publications, Inc., 31 East 2nd St., Mineola, N.Y. 11501. Dover publishes more than 400 books each year on science, elementary and advanced mathematics, biology, music, art, literary history, social sciences and other areas.

HOW TO WRITE, Gertrude Stein. Gertrude Stein claimed anyone could understand her unconventional writing—here are clues to help. Fascinating improvisations, language experiments, explanations illuminate Stein's craft and the art of writing. Total of 414pp. 4⅝ × 6⅜. 23144-5 Pa. $6.95

ADVENTURES AT SEA IN THE GREAT AGE OF SAIL: Five Firsthand Narratives, edited by Elliot Snow. Rare true accounts of exploration, whaling, shipwreck, fierce natives, trade, shipboard life, more. 33 illustrations. Introduction. 353pp. 5⅜ × 8½. 25177-2 Pa. $9.95

THE HERBAL OR GENERAL HISTORY OF PLANTS, John Gerard. Classic descriptions of about 2,850 plants—with over 2,700 illustrations—includes Latin and English names, physical descriptions, varieties, time and place of growth, more. 2,706 illustrations. xlv + 1,678pp. 8½ × 12¼. 23147-X Cloth. $89.95

DOROTHY AND THE WIZARD IN OZ, L. Frank Baum. Dorothy and the Wizard visit the center of the Earth, where people are vegetables, glass houses grow and Oz characters reappear. Classic sequel to *Wizard of Oz*. 256pp. 5⅜ × 8.
24714-7 Pa. $5.95

SONGS OF EXPERIENCE: Facsimile Reproduction with 26 Plates in Full Color, William Blake. This facsimile of Blake's original "Illuminated Book" reproduces 26 full-color plates from a rare 1826 edition. Includes "The Tyger," "London," "Holy Thursday," and other immortal poems. 26 color plates. Printed text of poems. 48pp. 5¼ × 7. 24636-1 Pa. $3.95

SONGS OF INNOCENCE, William Blake. The first and most popular of Blake's famous "Illuminated Books," in a facsimile edition reproducing all 31 brightly colored plates. Additional printed text of each poem. 64pp. 5¼ × 7.
22764-2 Pa. $3.95

PRECIOUS STONES, Max Bauer. Classic, thorough study of diamonds, rubies, emeralds, garnets, etc.: physical character, occurrence, properties, use, similar topics. 20 plates, 8 in color. 94 figures. 659pp. 6⅛ × 9¼.
21910-0, 21911-9 Pa., Two-vol. set $21.90

ENCYCLOPEDIA OF VICTORIAN NEEDLEWORK, S. F. A. Caulfeild and Blanche Saward. Full, precise descriptions of stitches, techniques for dozens of needlecrafts—most exhaustive reference of its kind. Over 800 figures. Total of 679pp. 8⅛ × 11. 22800-2, 22801-0 Pa., Two-vol. set $26.90

THE MARVELOUS LAND OF OZ, L. Frank Baum. Second Oz book, the Scarecrow and Tin Woodman are back with hero named Tip, Oz magic. 136 illustrations. 287pp. 5⅜ × 8½. 20692-0 Pa. $5.95

WILD FOWL DECOYS, Joel Barber. Basic book on the subject, by foremost authority and collector. Reveals history of decoy making and rigging, place in American culture, different kinds of decoys, how to make them, and how to use them. 140 plates. 156pp. 7⅞ × 10¾. 20011-6 Pa. $14.95

HISTORY OF LACE, Mrs. Bury Palliser. Definitive, profusely illustrated chronicle of lace from earliest times to late 19th century. Laces of Italy, Greece, England, France, Belgium, etc. Landmark of needlework scholarship. 266 illustrations. 672pp. 6⅛ × 9¼. 24742-2 Pa. $16.95

THE ART NOUVEAU STYLE BOOK OF ALPHONSE MUCHA: All 72 Plates from "Documents Decoratifs" in Original Color, Alphonse Mucha. Rare copyright-free design portfolio by high priest of Art Nouveau. Jewelry, wallpaper, stained glass, furniture, figure studies, plant and animal motifs, etc. Only complete one-volume edition. 80pp. 9⅜ × 12¼. 24044-4 Pa. $10.95

ANIMALS: 1,419 Copyright-Free Illustrations of Mammals, Birds, Fish, Insects, Etc., edited by Jim Harter. Clear wood engravings present, in extremely lifelike poses, over 1,000 species of animals. One of the most extensive pictorial source-books of its kind. Captions. Index. 284pp. 9 × 12. 23766-4 Pa. $10.95

OBELISTS FLY HIGH, C. Daly King. Masterpiece of American detective fiction, long out of print, involves murder on a 1935 transcontinental flight—"a very thrilling story"—*NY Times.* Unabridged and unaltered republication of the edition published by William Collins Sons & Co. Ltd., London, 1935. 288pp. 5⅜ × 8½. (Available in U.S. only) 25036-9 Pa. $5.95

VICTORIAN AND EDWARDIAN FASHION: A Photographic Survey, Alison Gernsheim. First fashion history completely illustrated by contemporary photographs. Full text plus 235 photos, 1840–1914, in which many celebrities appear. 240pp. 6½ × 9¼. 24205-6 Pa. $8.95

THE ART OF THE FRENCH ILLUSTRATED BOOK, 1700–1914, Gordon N. Ray. Over 630 superb book illustrations by Fragonard, Delacroix, Daumier, Doré, Grandville, Manet, Mucha, Steinlen, Toulouse-Lautrec and many others. Preface. Introduction. 633 halftones. Indices of artists, authors & titles, binders and provenances. Appendices. Bibliography. 608pp. 8⅜ × 11¼. 25086-5 Pa. $24.95

THE WONDERFUL WIZARD OF OZ, L. Frank Baum. Facsimile in full color of America's finest children's classic. 143 illustrations by W. W. Denslow. 267pp. 5⅜ × 8½. 20691-2 Pa. $7.95

FOLLOWING THE EQUATOR: A Journey Around the World, Mark Twain. Great writer's 1897 account of circumnavigating the globe by steamship. Ironic humor, keen observations, vivid and fascinating descriptions of exotic places. 197 illustrations. 720pp. 5⅜ × 8½. 26113-1 Pa. $15.95

THE FRIENDLY STARS, Martha Evans Martin & Donald Howard Menzel. Classic text marshalls the stars together in an engaging, nontechnical survey, presenting them as sources of beauty in night sky. 23 illustrations. Foreword. 2 star charts. Index. 147pp. 5⅜ × 8½. 21099-5 Pa. $3.95

FADS AND FALLACIES IN THE NAME OF SCIENCE, Martin Gardner. Fair, witty appraisal of cranks, quacks, and quackeries of science and pseudoscience: hollow earth, Velikovsky, orgone energy, Dianetics, flying saucers, Bridey Murphy, food and medical fads, etc. Revised, expanded In the Name of Science. "A very able and even-tempered presentation."—*The New Yorker.* 363pp. 5⅜ × 8.
20394-8 Pa. $6.95

ANCIENT EGYPT: Its Culture and History, J. E. Manchip White. From pre-dynastics through Ptolemies: society, history, political structure, religion, daily life, literature, cultural heritage. 48 plates. 217pp. 5⅜ × 8½. 22548-8 Pa. $5.95